Bernstein Pioneers

Descendants of
Julius (Judah) Bernstein
1789-1868

trudy chiswell
trudychiswell@gmail.com

 FriesenPress

One Printers Way
Altona, MB R0G 0B0
Canada

www.friesenpress.com

Research Collaborator: Miles Krisman: milez@rogers.com
Collaborators: Gerry Michaud, James Andrews, Henry Milling Bernstein
Photo Editor: Eileen Moore Crispin
Cover Art: Matthew Caryl

Disclaimer: All data in this book has been research to the most accurate current knowledge available. Special effort was made to confirm dates with hard data as much as possible.

ISBN
978-1-03-912481-3 (Hardcover)
978-1-03-912480-6 (Paperback)
978-1-03-912482-0 (eBook)

1. REFERENCE, GENEALOGY & HERALDRY

Distributed to the trade by The Ingram Book Company

TABLE OF CONTENTS

Introduction

*"To know nothing of the past, is to understand little of the present
and to have no concept of the future." ~ author unknown*

The journey of the Bernstein family is compiled from numerous stories gathered from family members, Ancestry.ca, and various online research sites over the past fifty years.[1] I'm the granddaughter of Charlotte Bernstein, great-granddaughter of Albert Manassas Bernstein, great-great-granddaughter of Phillip Bernstein, and great-great-great-granddaughter of Julius Bernstein. New information has come to light since my cousin Miles Krisman wrote the story of the Bernstein family about twenty-five years ago. Dates have been corrected or added since new hard data has become available, but this book would not have been possible without Miles' initial research and photocopied book he made available to the family.

I began this journey of tracking family lines when I was in my twenties just out of curiosity about my grandmother, who lived with us. I loved my Grannie Daley and started asking questions about her history. Sometimes I would get a response like, "Those are skeletons in the closet, and that is where we are going to leave them." It seemed to be the response of that generation regarding the parts of their lives they weren't happy about. Then I expanded my queries to her sisters, whom we visited on occasion. My curiosity grew over the years to researching in the library on microfiche and ordering my grandmother's birth and marriage certificates from the government. Everything was leg work back then. The urge to know my past grew exponentially when I discovered online research with the Ancestry program around 2003. Now at seventy-seven, I've decided that it's time to publish my research for the next generation to carry on.

I remember when I was twelve and my father visited his Bernstein cousins when he went to play his big sousaphone in a brass band at the New Orleans, Louisiana Mardi Gras parade. Oh, how I would love to have been with him with the knowledge I now have of the Bernstein family! With the limited travel bans of the COVID-19 pandemic in effect, I still can't go down and meet all the interesting people I've met via phone and email. Hopefully soon!

Since DNA testing became so available and easy to access, I've been put in touch with many distant relatives who helped me acquire information and photos for this book. Without them, the visual part of our past would be boring. It took a community to gather the information and photos to create this book. I feel more like a gatherer of information than a writer with this book. It's my hope that this book will be a jumping off place for many of you to follow your own family line and track current family history. Living generations are not included in the book unless the person has given specific permission. Being very aware of the prevalent issue of identity theft in today's world, I have left them out. I hope you enjoy looking at the people who blazed the trail of history before us.

NOTE: Names of my direct descendants are in red throughout the book.

Bernstein

Henry Chiswell
B: 01 Apr 1862 Ontario, Canada
M: 01 Jul 1885 Ontario, Canada
D: 16 Jul 1940 New York, USA

William Keal Chiswell
B: 17 February, 1811 England
D: 16 Feb 1896 Ontario, Canada

Sarah Ann Pike
B: 19 Nov 1820 Bristol, England
D: 25 Oct 1893 Ontario, Canada

Aubrey Reginald Chiswell UE
B: 3 Jul 1887 Ontario, Canada
M: 6 Feb 1910 Ontario, Canada
D: 28 Sep 1946 Ontario, Canada

Edith Alberta Smith UE
B: 14 Jan 1866 Ontario, Canada
M: 01 Jul 1885 Ontario, Canada
D: 11 Mar 1917 New York, USA

John Paul Smith UE
B: 5 April 1820 Ontario, Canada
D: 9 Oct 1871 Ontario, Canada

Mary Jane Marlatt
B: 3 Nov 1831 Beamsville, Ontario
D: 5 May 1880 Ontario, Canada

Albert Reginald Chiswell
B: March 11, 1911 Ontario, Canada
M: 21 Sept, 1935 Capreal, Ontario, Canada
D: 19 Apr 1969 Ontario, Canada

Albert Manassas Bernstein M.D.
B: 11 Mar 1862 Louisiana, USA
M: 18 Oct, 1882
D: 09 July 1897 Louisiana, USA

Phillip Bernstein
B: 10 April 1827 Poland
D: 7 July 1911 United States

Rosalia Budislofski Marx (Marks)
B: 10 May 1840 Germany
D: 05 May 1931 Louisiana, USA

Charlotte Imelda Bernstein (Chisw...
B: 13 Oct 1892 Louisiana, USA
M: 6 Feb 1910 Ontario, Canada
D: 7 Jan 1960 Ontario, Canada

F Moseley (Bernstein /Labelle)
B: 22 Sep 1866 Alabama, USA
M: 18 Oct, 1882
D: 31 Jul 1950 Ontario, Canada

William Jordan Moseley
B: 19 Apr 1840 Alabama, USA
D: 6 Jun 1896 United States

Sophronia Goodwin (Moseley)
B: abt 1847 Alabama
D: after 1880

trudy chiswell
B: 25 September 1943 Coniston, Greater Sudbury, O...
M: 20 Apr 1962 St Catharines, Niagara, Ontario, Can...
D: Living

Thomas J Daley
B: 24 DEC 1861 Ontario, Canada
M: 28 Apr 1889 Ontario, Canada
D: 17 FEB 1922 Ontario, Canada

Thomas Daley
B: 1831 Cork City, Cork, Ireland
D: 9 May 1914 , England

Mary O Dary Daley
B: abt 1836 County Cork, Ireland
D: 2 Mar 1921 United States

Michael Peter Daley
B: 16 Apr 1890 Ontario, Canada
M: 2 May 1916 Ontario, Canada
D: 7 Sep 1965 Ontario, Canada

Catherine O Gorman
B: 29 Jun 1861 Renfrew, Canada,
M: 28 Apr 1889 Ontario, Canada
D: 3 Sep 1933 Ontario, Canada

Daniel O'Gorman / Gorman
B: 1825 Knockerra, Clare, Ireland
D: 26 November 1901 Canada

Catherine O Reilly
B: 1827 Ireland
D: 1 Feb 1898 Ontario, Canada

Mary Margeory Veronica Daley
B: 12 Jan 1917 Pembroke, Ontario, Canada
M: 21 Sept, 1935 Capreal, Ontario, Canada
D: 3 Jan 1982 Ontario, Canada

Albert Gustave Maves
B: 3 Sep 1857 Prussia
M: 15 Feb 1882 Canada
D: Nov 8, 1919 Ontario, Canada

Frederick Gottlieb Maves
B: 1819 Prussia), Germany
D: 17 Mar 1879 Ontario, Canada

Frederike M. Keitter (Kaeter)
B: 10 July 1812 Germany
D: 3 Jul 1912 Ontario, Canada

Rosanna Nellie Maves
B: 30 Oct 1886 Ontario, Canada
M: 2 May 1916 Ontario, Canada
D: 2 Nov 1983 Ontario, Canada

Bertha Pauline Goldt
B: 22 Mar 1864 Ontario
M: 15 Feb 1882 Canada
D: 3 Jan 1936 Ontario, Canada

Carl August Ferdenald Goldt
B: 24 Dec 1833 Germany
D: 08 Apr 1915 Ontario, Canada

Adaline Caroline Rahn
B: 25 Nov 1832 Bayern, Germany
D: 28 Aug 1926 Ontario, Canada

What's in a Name?

Meaning of the name Bernstein

Bernstein = "Amber, the bear's stone"

Bernstein is a Jewish (Ashkenazic) and German name. It was originally taken from the German word "Bernstein," which means amber. That was derived from the Middle Low German words *bernen*, meaning to burn, and *stein*, meaning stone (amber was thought to be made by burning). It could also have been a locational name taken from a German town named Bernstein. Bernstein family history begins in Prussia, where they'd held political influence since ancient times. Most surnames are derived either from occupations or from geographical origin. They became heritable with the beginning of central demographic records in the early modern period.

Before the 1800s in Germany, the use of a surname by Jews was left to the discretion of the individual. Jews in Germany followed the custom of using only a given name and the name of the father, such as Isaac, son of Abraham (Isaac ben Abraham). Most Jews did not adopt hereditary family names until required to do so by law. By the 1820s, most small German states had extended civil rights to Jews and required them to adopt surnames. Now it makes sense why Phillip Bernstein's wife, Rosalia Budislofski, used her father's first name, Marks, as a surname when arriving in America.

Early History

In the medieval era, after the fall of the Roman Empire, the German lands were inhabited by a variety of tribes. The Bernstein surname was first found in Prussia, where the name was anciently associated with the tribal conflicts of the area. The borders of the kingdom changed frequently through war, and the Bernstein's contributions were sought by many leaders in their search for power. Reformation was introduced into Prussia in 1486, a religious revolution that swept through Europe. The majority of Prussian subjects were therefore Lutherans, while the Jewish Bernsteins were Ashkenazic Jewish. During a period of change in the country in 1701, when Frederick I crowned himself King of Prussia, the family moved to Prussia taking the Bernstein name with them, where they became more entrenched as one of the notable family names of the region. They established several branch houses of the name, and some were not confined to the region. Many migrated to capitalize on their interests in religious, military, or political service.

Symbolism of the Family Coat of Arms

Family crests and coats of arms are powerful family symbols passed down through generations. The symbolism in the design of a family crest or coat of arms can tell you about your ancestors' achievements and status in society—a real testament to a family's legacy. In the feudal states of the Holy Roman Empire, which at one time encompassed most of Eastern Europe, it was especially important to be able to differentiate enemies from allies because of the many conflicts that occurred there. A system of heraldry evolved that achieved this. It regulated what arms were borne and allowed each of the German knights to be distinguishable from others.

Colors and symbol meanings of the Bernstein Family Crest

- Gold: generosity and elevation of the mind
- Red: warrior or martyr, military strength and magnanimity
- Black: constancy or grief, or winter
- Lion: dauntless courage

The helmet, or helm, is an Esquire's Helm facing to its right. On top of the helmet is a torse, or wreath, which was formed by two pieces of silk twisted together to hold the crest and mantle on the helm. [2]

Life before Coming to America

What was life like for our ancestors before they came to America? I wondered what life was like in Gnesen, Posen, Prussia to cause an entire family to immigrate to America. Why would my great-grandfather, Phillip Bernstein, run away to England when he was eleven years old?

In the first half of the thirteenth century, when the Germans crossed the frontier and began to settle in the territory of Posen, a large number of Jews came with them. Even before that time, however, Jews were living in Great Poland.

Gnesen (now called Gniezno), Posen, Prussia is a town in central-western Poland (now), about fifty kilometers (thirty-one miles) east of Pozanan. One of the oldest towns in the former kingdom of Poland (1025–1385), it is in an undulating and fertile country. After a long period of decay, the town revived after 1815 when it came under the rule of Prussia. It was Poland's most ancient capital. In the 1800s Prussian educational system remained the best in Europe, with the University of Berlin enjoying an unrivaled reputation.

Life in old Gnesen, Prussia (Gniezno in current Poland)

Jewish Life in Prussia

According to a legendary account, a synagogue existed in Gnesen as early as 1582. The Ashkenazy Jews are people of the Jewish faith, and their ancestors lived in the Rhine Valley and in neighboring France before their migration eastward to the Slavic lands of Poland, Lithuania, and Russia after the Crusades. After the seventeenth-century persecutions in Eastern Europe, large numbers of these Jews resettled in

Western Europe, where they assimilated with other Jewish communities. Today, Ashkenazim constitutes more than 80 percent of all the Jews in the world.

In the twelfth century, Jews were employed at Gnesen as farmers of mint and as coiners. The inscriptions on these coins are partly in pure Hebrew and partly in Polish. By the fourteenth century, Jews were permitted to acquire land, a privilege that was subsequently repealed, and women as well as men engaged in money lending. The Jews followed many callings at this time: tailors, furriers, bakers, braiders, butchers, glaziers, tanners, barbers, goldsmiths, gold-embroiderers, gold-refiners, jewelers, button-makers, cap-makers, seal-engravers, silk-dyers, horn-workers, cooks, porters, or musicians. I'm curious if the Bernsteins had a tailor shop, as four of the brothers who came to America worked as tailors at some point. Immigrating to America in 1847, Isaac Bernstein opened a famous tailor/clothier store in New York that continued on through at least two more generations that I know of.

Increased contact with Western languages, manners, and customs came to the Ashkenazy people only in the eighteenth century, when new economic opportunities created such possibilities. Jewish bankers, brokers, army suppliers, and capitalists were permitted to live in places such as Berlin because they opened new factories or were otherwise helpful to the expansion of the economy.

Jewish Persecution

The Jews of Poland were not exempt from persecution, which generally occurred in times of war or economic depression. Social oppressions were frequently caused by the Catholic clergy and the German merchants for religious and commercial reasons. In 1654, Jesuit students plundered the Jews' street of Gnesen, and two years later some Jews were slain.

1648–1790—Polish Jews suffered terribly during the peasant revolts of 1648–1790 involving Poland, Russia, and Sweden. The Jews were slaughtered by rebels and professional soldiers, and many survivors were sold as slaves in Turkey.

1793—In this year, when the Prussians took possession of Poland, there were fifty-three tailors, ten butchers, and six furriers. By 1800, the Jewish population of Gnesen had increased to 761, and by 1815, there were 4,223 Jews, or 6.5 percent of the population of Gnesen.

A Warring Nation

Prussia was a warring nation, constantly at war with neighbors or with civil uprisings.

1797–1840—Frederick William III at first pursued a foreign policy of caution and neutrality with respect to France and Napoleon I during his reign in Poland.

1806—October 14, 1806, was the military engagement of the Napoleonic Wars. Napoleon smashed the outdated Prussian army and reduced the size of Prussia by half if its former size in the treaty of Tilsit in July 1807. This produced a shifting of alliances of European powers that gave a brief French dominance over most of Europe.

Napoleon emancipated the Jews and introduced other ideas of freedom from the French Revolution. He overrode old laws restricting Jews to reside in ghettos as well as lifted laws that limited Jews' rights to property, worship, and certain occupations. However, he also restricted the Jewish practice of money lending, restricted the regions to which Jews were allowed to migrate, and required Jews to adopt formal names (see previous article on "What is in a Name").

1812—Prussia was forced to send auxiliary troops for Napoleon's campaign in Russia.

Julius Bernstein, 1789–1868 (my great-great-great-grandfather), was a surgeon in the Napoleonic Wars.

1813–14—War of Liberation. The reformed Prussian army drove Napoleon into exile on Elba Island, a tiny island of eighty-six square miles off the coast of Italy.

1815—The Grand Duchy of Posen was annexed by Prussia in the Polish partitions of 1815. Three partitions were redrawn. The Austrians established Glaicia, and the Russians gained Warsaw from Prussia, which became the Province of Posen in the Kingdom of Prussia in 1848. Gnesen is the red dot on the following map of Poland.

The Poles staged uprisings in 1806, 1830, 1846, and 1848. Defeats were followed by "organic work" that aimed at strengthening the society and its economy by peaceful means.

1834—Prussia took the lead in the economic unification of Germany.

1848—March–May 1848 was The Greater Poland uprising. It was an unsuccessful military insurrection of Poles again Prussian forces that resulted in a Prussian victory. The Prussian bureaucracy established a high standard of efficiency and honesty that was at this time unique to Europe.

By 1842, the Bernstein family started immigrating to America one by one, starting with the oldest son, Samuel. As you can see, Germany/Prussia was constantly at war, and I can understand why my great-great-grandfather, Phillip Bernstein, 1827–1911, ran away to England at eleven years old. His father was probably away at war as a military surgeon, and he could see the writing on the wall of his future—to be conscripted into the army at some point. We don't know at this point what happened to the five children that died in Prussia before 1857 and didn't immigrate to America. Were they killed in one of the wars or uprisings, or did they die of disease? Those are still mysteries to explore. [3]

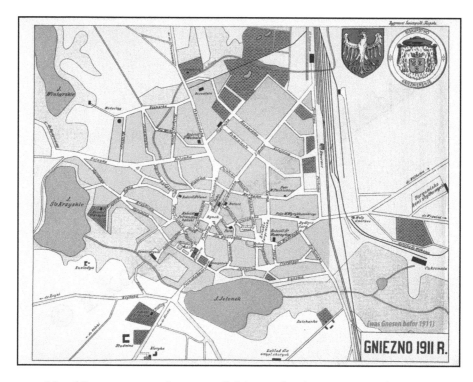

Map of Gniezno in 1911—the city was called Gnesen when the Bernsteins were living there

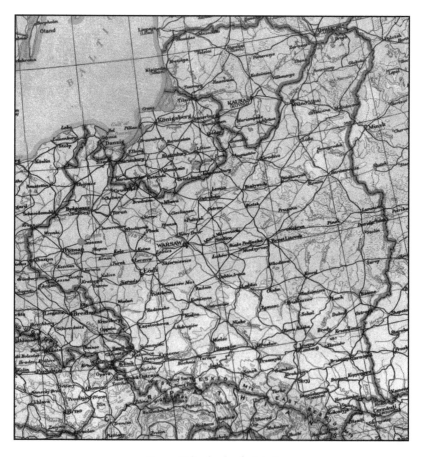

Gnesen Poland today (red dot)

Jewish Roots

When I started researching my ancestry roots, I discovered that I come from Jewish roots in the Bernstein family. I became more and more curious as to what that meant and what defined the Jewish faith. On my research journey, I stumbled upon a gentleman who'd left a memorial on findagrave.com site for one of my great-grandfather's brothers. James Andrews is retired from the US Army and currently a legal professional, a genealogist, a geneticist, and also a Jew. James has been very generous in answering all my questions about DNA and the Jewish faith. From the Bernstein's DNA, we apparently descend from the tribe of Levi in the Bible and later acquired the designation of Ashkenazi Jews because the family originated from Eastern Europe. I study the Bible and thought that was pretty cool! One famous Ashkenazi Jew was Albert Einstein.

Judaism dates back nearly four thousand years and is documented in the Old Testament of the Bible. Followers believe in one God, who revealed himself through ancient prophets. It's a rich heritage of law, culture, and tradition. Judaism is defined as the totality of beliefs and practices of the Jewish people, as given by God and recorded in the Torah and subsequently the Tanakh. Today there are about fourteen million Jews worldwide, with most of them living in the United States and Israel.

The Jewish DNA

By James Andrews: Lawyer, Genealogist, Geneticist
james_andrews555@yahoo.com

Bernstein DNA

The Bernstein DNA lineage and the presentation of J-CTS as a haplogroup finding in the male line is assigned to J-M304. The Ashkenazi Jews were Jewish prior to regional migration and marriage into Poland, Russia, and Turkey. They received the Ashkenazim designation after they began migrating into those regions. They were Jewish people with ancient origin prior to any regional migration. The J1 and J2 Y-DNA are designated as High Priest, Priest DNA. J-M267 is the only known male-passed Jewish (Hebrew) gene, a requirement based on Halakhic Law that Levitical Priests must have a direct-paternal descent from Aaron, the brother of Moses. Aaron was the Patriarch of the Tribe of Levi, having a direct descendant Zadok. Without exception, all High Priests must have male-passed J-M267 genetics.

Your Bernstein DNA lineage indicated that you descend from an intermarriage to the tribe of Levi and subsequent inter-genetic distribution of the J1 DNA.

Origin of DNA

G_d designated mankind, in all ways, as an individual genetic expression of the direct creation by G_d. Our human expression, down to the cellular level, at a mitochondrial origin is the will of G_d. Our quest for detailed knowledge on where we came from can only be achieved through a complete acceptance that G_d's perfection in creation can never be concealed. It is through man's disagreement, inferior understanding, and corrupted configuration that our true origin gets inaccurately interpreted.

Modern-day science continues to produce greater and greater genetic expression and superior methodology in DNA determination. While all this rapidly expanding science has given us greater knowledge of our origin, the key to creative perfection originates from G_d and is displayed within us.

All of us, Jew and non-Jew.

No amount of diaspora or dispersion can diminish this fact.

The Jewish Faith and DNA

The Jewish faith is a historical, literary, and lineage-based faith rooted in the Torah and the Talmud. It is a combination of people who are diaspora-displaced or wandering. Moreover, the displacement is the plight of God's Chosen People through the trials and tribulations of humanity. The Jewish faith is within the people, or the Chosen People of God from Israel, who were dispersed throughout the earth. The commonality, or common goal, is their worship of God, respect for his laws, and obedience to rabbinical law. God is referred to as G_d out of respect for his holiness and sacredness.

An interesting point is that no major world religion exists without either basis in or through the Hebrew origins of Judaism. The works of the Jewish people are the basis for Christianity more than non-Jewish people recognize. My Earliest Known Descendant, or EKA, was Moricius Andresys; his advanced DNA designations (through myself and other descendants) provides a paternal DNA designation of J-M267.

The J-M267 Y-DNA shows an origin to Azerbaijan from a DNA intersect at modern day Belarus. The DNA origin is from a migratory pathway traveled from Palestine and Iraq. The J-M267 DNA is uniquely and conclusively traceable from Zadok, the High Priest of the Tribe of Levi. Zadok was grandson to Aaron, the brother of Moses, and direct patrilineal descendant to Phineas. The Kohen Gadol, or High Priest, is anointed to be the leader of the brethren. The Kohen Model that diagrams this is found to produce distinct Y-DNA pattern distribution.

The J-M267 male-passed DNA is designated to/through the Prophet Muhammad through the German, Luxembourg Grand Dynasties, to the Wales and Tudor lineage, and, in the British Isles, to the Andrewes lines. Lancelot Andrewes, a very well-respected Anglican bishop in Great Britain, was tasked by King James in 1604 to interpret and translate the Bible from the Greek and Hebrew to the (KJV) King James Version Bible. King James did this to settle some thorny religious differences in his kingdom and solidify his own supremacy.

Lancelot Andrewes was a Jew by lineage if not by formal practice, but his devotion to Hebraic interpretation is very telling. He was devout to God and knew well the Torah, the Talmud, and Kabbalah practices. Born in 1555, he was well respected and widely known for his astute theological interpretation and multi-linguistic interpretational work. Another J-M267 designee, William Tyndale, shared a cousinship to Lancelot Andrewes; his version of translation preceded Lancelot's KJV Bible.

The Bible and the Talmud vary greatly. There is more expansive accounting, lineage, and history in the Talmud. The Talmud is the written, paraphrased, and rabbinical instruction of the Torah. The Torah is the documented historical passages that were passed through the ages while maintaining strict doctrinal focus. The Torah is "God's words" (the teaching), and the Talmud are "God's words specifically for his Chosen People (perspective of those teachings)."

The Shem genealogy records you have in the Christian Bible, and the one I have been taught, contrast each other. This is attributable to different religious-specific sources, non-Hebrew opinion of Hebraic origin, and other theories. The Torah certainly differs from the Bible accounting, although the biblical illustration is based on the Torah, but it does not give greater description or instruction than is necessitated by Hebraic Law. This is applicable to genealogy as much as any other aspect of historical, religious, or esoteric description of God's Chosen People. All advanced geneticists agree that from Adam to Noah there was much more than Seth's DNA preserved, distributed, and genetically accounted for. This is the basis for Hebraic Priesthood, the leaders of the Tribes of Judah, and the hierarchy of the structure in our synagogues. [4]

ℭℬ ℭℬ ℭℬ

THE
BERNSTEIN STORIES

Julius (Judah) & Bertha Bernstein ~ Family Chart

Julius (Judah) Bernstein 1859

Julius (Judah) Bernstein
b. Feb 15, 1789 Gnesen, Posen, Prussia
d. Mar 10, 1868, Kingston, NY USA
m. 1815 in Gniezno, Poland
Bertha Yehetshi Bernstein *(12 children)*
b. Jan 2, 1796 Posen, Prussia
d. Jan 8, 1876, Kingston, NY USA

Bertha Bernstein 1859

Samuel Bernstein
b. June 3, 1816 Gnesen, Posen, Prussia
d. Aug 29, 1900, Montgomery, Louisiana, US
Occupation: Dry Goods Merchant

Married ~ Charlotte Yehetshi
b. Aug 3, 1818, Posen, Prussia
d. June 3, 1888, Montgomery, Louisiana US
m. July 27, 1842, Gnesen, Posen, Prussia

No children

Isaac Bernstein
b. Apr 10, 1818, Gnesen, Posen, Prussia
d. Mar 29, 1897, Kingston, New York
Occupation: Tailor

Married ~ Henrietta Bernstein
b. Apr 1, 1824, Prussia
d. Mar 13, 1918, Manhattan, New York, US
m. 1851 place not known

1. Abraham 1849-1903 (m.Addie Weiner)
2. Pauline ˙852-1864 (died at 12)
3. Henry 1854-1935 (bachelor)
4. Augusta B. 1857-1926 (m.Richard Weiner)
5. Alexander 1859-1924 (m. Salome Cohen)
6. Isabella 1860-1934 (m.David Fink)
7. Samuel ˙862-1935 (m. Martha Manner)
8. Flora 1864-1936 (spinster)
9. Jacob 1866-1952 (m. Grace Eunist)

Robert Bernstein - bachelor
b. abt. 1821 Gnesen, Posen, Prussia

Gustav Bernstein - bachelor
b. abt. 1824 Gnesen, Posen, Prussia
d. before 1857 Gnesen, Posen, Prussia

Phillip Berstein
b. Apr 10, 1827, Posen, Prussia
d. Jul 7, 1911, Winnfield, Louisiana US
Occupation: Dry Good Merchant

Married ~ Rosalia Budislofski (Marks)
b. May 10, 1840 Gnesen, Posen, Prussia
d. May 5, 1931 Winnfield, Louisiana US
m. Jul 12, 1859, Montgomery, Louisiana US

1. Dr. Albert Manassas1862-1897 (Florence Moseley)
2. Henry 1863-1931 (m.Cherry Roberts)
3. Augusta 1865-1867 - spinster
4. Julian 1868-1941 - bachelor
4. Rudolph 1870-1948 (m.Alice Leopold)
5. Nettie (Tulla) 1872-1959 - spinster
6. Isaac 1873-1921 - bachelor
7. Arnold 1374-1937 (m.Corinne Steinau)
8. Bertha 1876-1936 (m. Marcus Kaliski)

Augusta Bernstein - spinster
b. abt. 1831 Gnesen, Posen, Prussia
d. Sept 19, 1853 Pineville, Louisiana US
- *died of yellow fever shortly after arriving to the US*

Morris Bernstein - bachelor
b. Oct 4, 1834 Gnesen, Posen, Prussia
d. June 6, 1918 Winnfield, Louisiana US
Occupation: Dry goods store merchant

Rebecca Bernstein - spinster
b. abt. 1836 Genesen, Posen, Prussia
d. before 1857 Genesen, Posen, Prussia

Adolph Bernstein - bachelor
b. abt. 1838 Genesen, Posen, Prussia
d. before 1857 Genesen, Posen, Prussia

Mary Bernstein - spinster??
b. abt 1840 Genesen, Posen, Prussia
d. ???

Joseph Bernstein - Confederate Army 1861-65
b. Aug 20, 1841, Genesen, Posen, Prussia
d. abt 1910 Coushatta, Louisiana US
Occupation: postmaster & hotel operator

Married ~ Jeanette Budislofski (Marks)
b. Dec 1846, Prussia
d. Aug 23, 1912, Coushatta, Louisiana US
m. Nov 27, 1873, Montgomery, Louisiana US

1. Eugene 1876-1955 - bachelor
2. Leon 1379-1927 (m. Minnie Devlin)
3. Jeanie Rena 1880-1926 - bachelor
4. Beatrice 1881-1962 - spinster

Source of information Miles Krisman, Gerry Michaud & Ancestry.ca

compiled by trudy chiswell- trudychiswell@fastmail.fm &[Date]

Julius (Judah) Bernstein: 1789–1868

Immigrated to the US in 1857

My earliest known descendant in the Bernstein family is Julius Bernstein, 1789–1868. Julius Bernstein is my great-great-great-grandfather, father of Phillip Bernstein, who settled in Winnfield, Louisiana. Phillip was the father of Albert Manassas Bernstein, my great-grandfather. My grandmother was one of Albert Manassas's six children. The Bernsteins had an interesting history and became prominent contributors to their community.

Julius was born February 15, 1789. He married Bertha, who was born January 2, 1796, in Posen, Saale-Holzland-Kreis, Thueringen, Prussia. The couple married in 1815 in Gniezno, Poland. Both Julius and Bertha lived in the town of Gnesen (Gniezno in modern Poland) in the province of Posen, Prussia, which was the Prussian part of Poland. In an oral history dictated by his granddaughter Nettie in her twilight years, she shared that Julius had been a surgeon during the Franco-Prussian (Napoleon) war of 1806 in their homeland. When Poland was divided after this, Julius's part of the country became Prussia, while the other portions of Poland became Austrian and Russian. One cannot know in which army he served, as many Polish Prussians supported Napoleon.

The Jewish community in Gnesen had always been the smallest in the Polish Kingdom. At the end of the seventeenth century, it consisted of one hundred people in thirty houses. Local merchants dealt in wool rags and collected tolls. The synagogue was built in 1582. The Swedish war (1655–1659), combined with the attacks led by the Jesuits, resulted in the destruction of the community. In 1661, it reorganized outside the city walls. A new synagogue was built in 1680. In the first half of the eighteenth century, the community suffered during the Northern War, and there was an outbreak of fire. By 1744, there were only sixty Jews living in Gnesen. The community grew during the second half of the eighteenth century, particularly after Gnesen came under Prussian rule with the second partition of Poland in 1793. It grew from 251 people in the beginning of the period to 1,783 people by the middle of the nineteenth century.

Map of Prussia, 1862–1871   *Prussian Flag*

Julius and Bertha were living in Gnesen during the re-birth of the community. They themselves were to have eleven children; however, only six lived to maturity. The others died young (before 1857). Of these six children, all eventually made their way to the United States of America. In 1857, Julius, Bertha, and daughter Mary followed the sons to the US along with Rosalia (Budislofski) Marks, who was to marry their son Phillip. Mary later married a Mr. Pinner. The ancestral couple stayed and spent the rest of their lives with their son Isaac in Kingston, New York, where Isaac had a clothing manufacturing store. Rosalia went on to Louisiana to meet her husband-to-be.

Julius Bernstein died on March 17, 1868, and Bertha died January 7, 1876. Both are buried in Kingston, New York.

Julius and Bertha Bernstein's Children

1. Samuel, 1816–1900

2. Isaac, 1818–abt. 1897

3. Robert, 1821–abt. 1857

4. Gustave, 1824–abt. 1857

5. Phillip, 1827–1911

6. Augusta, 1831–1853

7. Morris, 1834–1918

8. Rebecca, 1836–abt. 1857

9. Adolph, 1838–abt. 1857

10. Mary, 1840–unknown

11. Joseph B., 1841–1910

Julius Bernstein, 1789–1868

Bertha Bernstein, 1796–1876

These paintings are of Bertha and Julius Bernstein, painted in 1859 by Thomas Lehman, New Orleans, and hung in Nettie Bernstein's home. Donated by her nephew Phillip Roby to Temple B'nai Israel in Monroe, Louisiana and graciously photographed by the temple historian, Sandra Blate. Used with permission of Temple B'nai Israel, where the paintings are now housed.

Samuel Bernstein: 1816–1900

Samuel Bernstein was a tailor. He married Charlotte Yehetski (Yachetsky), who was also born in Gnesen, Posen, Prussia. Her date of birth was August 3, 1818. Charlotte's sister, Rena Yehetski, married Marcus Budislofski. Two of their daughters were to marry into the Bernstein Family.

Immediately after their marriage in Gnesen, Samuel and Charlotte left for America. They are said to have embarked from Hamburg on July 27, 1842. After a voyage of sixty-two days, they landed at Castle Garden, New York. They made their home in New York until late 1845. Sam was a tailor when he arrived. Sam and Charlotte were the first of the family to go south when they arrived in New Orleans, Louisiana on September 27, 1845. In the spring of 1846, they moved on to Little Rock, Arkansas. In the fall of 1847, they moved to Pine Bluff, Arkansas. This was in the slave running days. In the spring of 1848, they returned to Rapides Parish, Louisiana. At little River, which was located at a point where Castor Creek and Desdemona River meet, they established a trading post. He had an Irishman and an Indian there for servants at the time.

About this time, Samuel's brother, Phillip, joined them. He worked as a peddler for them, travelling the state selling wares from a pack on his back. In addition to their merchandising business, they shipped pine knots to New Orleans to be used in the manufacturing of gas for streetlamps. They prospered in this business, and after a few years of running their trading post they moved to Alexandria and opened a store. Samuel and Charlotte Bernstein never had any children.

In 1856–1858, Samuel and Charlotte moved to Montgomery, now in Grant Parish, where they established another store. In 1863, they bought a farm across the river in Natchitoches (Ward 9) where they lived.

In July/August of 1859, after Phillip married, Samuel and Charlotte went to New York to see Samuels's parents, Julius and Bertha. While in New York, they had their portraits painted. (These portraits are currently in the home of Henry Milling Bernstein in Shreveport, Louisiana.) Charlotte bought four cake plates. One broke in her lifetime, and the other three today are in the homes of Phillip Bernstein's granddaughter, Rosalia Goldsmith.

This part of the United States was not yet well established, and it was still sparsely populated. Slave running was still a part of the frontier economy, and law and order weren't always maintained. In fact,

while riding a horse back to Alexandria, Charlotte came upon a duel in the woods in which both participants killed each other. This duel had apparently been brewing for some time, and each of the men had
sworn they would kill the other one when they met. They were both known to Charlotte, but she didn't
recall their names. Such was life on the frontier. For security, Samuel and Charlotte kept their money in
a nail keg. Business must have been quite good, for it's said that at the end of the day, Sam would scoop
the silver and gold coins with quart cups and drop them in Charlotte's lap to be separated and counted!
After a couple of years of running their trading post, they moved to Alexandria and opened a store.

Their store in Alexandria is said to have been located on the levee. Sam and Charlotte would have
been known in Alexandria prior to their locating there, as they had been bringing their merchandise for
the trading post from Alexandria. According to the 1850 census, the Jewish community of Alexandria
consisted of only about twenty-four individuals; this number understates the actual total, because there
was a transient population of peddlers. Still, the Jews represented only about half of one percent of the
then population of Rapides Parish, and 1.8 percent of the then city of Alexandria.

In 1866, Charlotte took sick; consequently, she and Sam sold their home in New Orleans and moved
back to Natchitoches Parish. There, on June 3, 1888, Charlotte (Yebetski) Bernstein died. She was
interred in the Jewish Cemetery in Pineville, Louisiana.

Samuel Bernstein remained on his farm of about two hundred acres for the rest of his life. On August
29, 1900, at the age of eighty-four, he died. His final days were spent across the river in Montgomery
at the home of his brother, Phillip. His remains were brought to Alexandria on the Texas and Pacific
Railroad and taken to the Masonic Hall on Third Street, where he had been a Worshipful Master of his
lodge many times. He was laid to rest beside his wife in the Jewish Cemetery in Pineville on August 30.
He was buried with Masonic honors.

Samuel Bernstein 1816-1900

BERNSTEIN.—At his home in Montgomery, Grant parish, La., on Wednesday, August 29, 1900, at 3 p. m., Samuel Bernstein, aged 84 years.

The remains were brought to Alexandria on the Texas and Pacific road, arriving this morning, and taken to the Masonic Hall on Third street, and buried with Masonic honors this afternoon in the cemetery, Pineville.

The deceased was born in Prussia Poland, Europe, and crossed the ocean to the United States in 1842. He went to New Orleans in 1845, and after a few years stay came to Alexandria in 1848, and lived here a number of years. In 1858 he moved to Montgomery and lived there up to the time of his death. His wife died in 1888. He leaves three brothers, viz: Phillip Bernstein, of Montgomery, at whose home he died; Morris Bernstein, of Winnfield, and Joe B. Bernstein, of Coushatta. He was a charter member of Oliver Lodge, No. 84, F. & A. M., of Alexandria.—Town Talk.

We are grieved to record the death of Uncle Sammy Bernstein. He was a great friend of this editor's honored father, and never failed to refer to his friendship whenever in our presence. Honorable, simple and kind hearted, he was loved and respected by all who knew him. Peace be to his memory.

Left to Right: Jeanette Budislofski—Rosalia Budislofski Marks (Phillip's wife) —Charlotte Yehetski Bernstein (Samuel's wife)

Samuel & Charlotte Bernstein graves in Pinesville, Rapides Parish, Louisiana

Life in Monroe, Louisiana in the 1800's

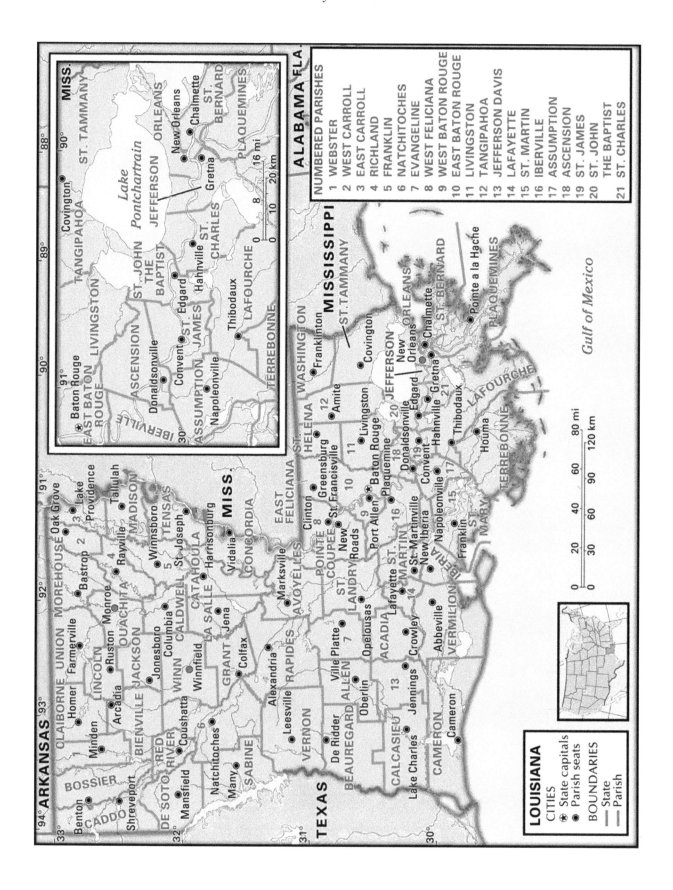

Isaac Bernstein: 1818–1897

The second child of Julius and Bertha Bernstein was Isaac. Isaac came to the United States of America in 1847. The earliest US census I have found was from October 14, 1850. In that record, Isaac lives in Kingston, New York, and is listed as a tailor at an apparel and accessory store. He is married to Henrietta, and his first child, Abraham, is one year old. His brother Morris is with him. A record from November 18, 1850, has Isaac with his older brother Samuel, thirty-three, his wife Charlotte, and his brother Phillip. Both Phillip and Isaac are listed as working as peddlers for Samuel's trading post.

In the 1860 census, Isaac is in Kingston, New York, and his real estate worth is $6,000 (abt. $97,500 in today's purchase power). His personal estate is worth $2,000. By the 1865 census, Isaac is still residing in Kingston, New York, listed as a clothing store owner, and with seven children. He had established a business at 86 North Front St. in Kingston, New York. He is described as a "merchant tailor and manufacturer of clothing." From another census, it appears that Isaac remained in Kingston, New York all his life. When his parents, Julius and Bertha Bernstein, immigrated to the US, they apparently lived with Isaac. In the 1870 census, Bertha is living with Isaac and his family of eight children, all born in New York.

Isaac and Henrietta's Children

1. Abraham, March 10, 1849–January 26, 1903

2. Pauline, August 14, 1852–March 31, 1864

3. Henry, June 13, 1854–September 3, 1935

4. Augusta, October 1857–February 5, 1926

5. Alexander, October 10, 1859–October 1, 1924

6. Isabella, March 1860–April 16, 1934

7. Samuel, February 1862–July 25, 1935

8. Flora, May 1864–September 17, 1936

9. Jacob, February 1866–February 14, 1952

Abraham: Abraham was a clerk with an occupation in the 1900 census as wholesale Lignors (something to do with the collection of wood). He married Addie Weiner (b. October 1855–1918) and had six children.

Pauline: Pauline died at thirteen years of age.

Henry: Henry stayed in Kingston but traveled to Kingston, Jamaica for a time. The census says he was brewery salesman, and it doesn't appear that he ever married.

Augusta: Augusta married Richard Weiner on October 6, 1881. He was born in April 1857, and it doesn't appear they had any children. They did have Augusta's mother, Henrietta, living with them in the 1900–1915 census in Manhattan, New York. It's believed that Henrietta lived with Augusta's family until her death on March 13, 1918. Flora, Augusta's sister, also lived with them until her death in 1936.

Alexander: Alexander moved to Portland, Oregon where he was a lawyer. He married Solome Solis Cohan in 1887, and they had three children: Leon, Judith, and Salome S.C. Salome married into the Cohen family in Portland, where they were well known for their early cinematography business and theatres. The 1900 census was taken at Good Samaritan Hospital, Portland, Oregon, so perhaps that was where he worked. Alexander is buried in the Beth Israel Jewish cemetery, Portland, Oregon.

Isabella: Isabella was a graduate of Kingston Academy, working as a teacher at school #8, Kingston, and then in 1920 as a social worker for the Red Cross. She married David Fink, a jewelry salesman and watch repairman around 1885 in New York. The couple had one son, Adrian, who became an engineer. Isabella's burial in Wiltwyck Cemetery, Kingston, New York, was attended by the rabbi of Temple Emanuel.

Samuel: Samuel when out West as a young man and is registered in Alameda, California as a salesman in 1894. He married Martha A. Maenner in 1886 in Multonomah, Oregon. Martha was born in June 1866 in Maryland. On November 12, 1889, their son Sam Jr. was born in Portland, Oregon, where Samuel's brother Alexander had a law practice. Samuel's father, Isaac, died on March 29, 1897, and by the 1900 census, Samuel has moved back to Kingston to look after the family business. I can't find a notation of when Samuel and his family came back to Kingston, New York, but by 1900 the family were living at 173 Pearl St, Kingston, New York, where they stayed until the 1920 census. Samuel is listed as a men's retail clothier. The family then moved to 231 Washington Ave., Kingston, New York.

Samuel took over his father's clothing business, which had relocated to 355 Wall St. in Kingston. By utilizing his experience and with much hard work, he built "Sam Bernstein & Co., Clothiers" into one of Kingston's largest business of that period. One of their slogans in a newspaper advertisement was, "Your Money's Worth or Your Money Back." As was typical of the Bernstein family, he also took a keen interest in his community and many charitable endeavors. He became a member and president of the Kingston Board of Education (elected 1916) and a bank trustee and official. He was active in Y.M.C.A. affairs, a member of Temple Emanuel of Rondout, and he helped establish the Ulster County Tuberculosis

Hospital. He was directly connected to all related charities and in all philanthropic circles. He was a leader in the Kingston Chamber of Commerce and advanced the city along prosperous and progressive lines. His death on July 25, 1935, was a great loss to his wife, family, and the entire city. Samuel was buried in Wiltwyck Cemetery, Kingston, New York.

His son, Samuel Bernstein Jr., followed in the footsteps of his father and further developed the Wall Street property into one of the most valuable sites and buildings in the Kingston shopping district, called Sam Bernstein & Co. Inc. It is still in operation today. Sam Jr. was drafted for WWII and registered as a manager for Sam Bernstein & Co. Inc. Sam Jr. had two children.

Samuel Bernstein Jr., 1889–1956

Flora: (May 1864–September 17, 1936) Flora never married and remained home with her parents until her father's death. Both Flora and her mother, Henrietta, moved in with Henrietta's sister Augusta and her husband, Richard Weiner, in Manhattan, New York. It appears that she worked at the Bernstein store for a period of time. Flora died on September 17, 1936, at seventy-two years of age, and is buried with her parents and brother Henry at the Wiltwyck Cemetery in Kingston, New York.

Jacob: (February 1866–February 14, 1952) Jacob married Grace Eunist in 1885 in Kingston, New York, and the couple had one son, Harold E., born March 19, 1897. Jacob is listed on many census records as a merchant tailor and salesman, so perhaps he worked in the Bernstein family store with his brother. Grace died on December 19, 1930, and Jacob died on February 14, 1952. Both are buried in the Wiltwyck Cemetery, Kingston, New York, where many of the extended family were also buried. Harold E. was in the Army in WWI and WWII. He didn't go overseas in WWI, and it's not known about his service in WWII.

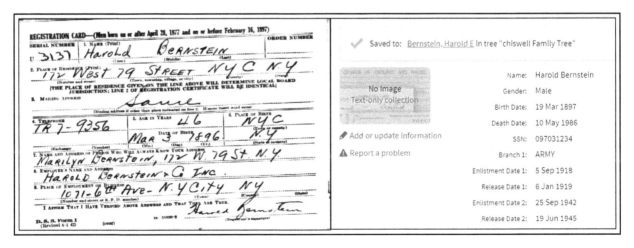

WWII registration & military record for Harold Bernstein

Isaac Bernstein 1818-1897

<table>
<tr><td>APPLICATION No. 162508</td><td>FILED AND MARRIAGE LICENSE ISSUED - September 9, 1921</td></tr>
</table>

Name Adrian B. Fink	Name Esther A. Weinstein
Age 28 Residence 409 Euclid Ave.	Age 23 Residence 10121 Pierpont Ave.
Place of Birth Providence, R. I.	Place of Birth Russia
Occupation Engineer	Occupation Clerk
Father's Name David C.	Father's Name Moses
Mother's Maiden Name Belle Bernstein	Mother's Maiden Name Toba Berger
Number of times previously married none	Number of times previously married none

Marriage to be solemnized by Rev. Rabbi Goldman, Cleveland, O. License issued by Frank Zizelman, Deputy Clerk
Consent of — Filed — 19 Consent of — Filed — 19

THE STATE OF OHIO, ss. RETURN
CUYAHOGA COUNTY.
I CERTIFY, That on the 11th day of September 1921, Mr. Adrian B. Fink
and Miss Esther A. Weinstein were by me legally joined in marriage.
Rev. Solomon Columan

Cohen, I. Leeser (1858-1943)

Brother of D.Solis Cohen, ~~and of Charney, Benjamin J. Cohen;~~ was associated with the former in the Portland firm of Cohen & Davis, merchants, in 1880s, 1890s.

Member of a colonial family of Philadelphia, of Sephardic-Jewish descent. (Cohen and Solis families)
Son of Myer David and Judith S. da Silva Solis Cohen. Brother also of Mrs. Alexander Bernstein (Salome Solis Cohen), wife of Portland attorney.
I. Leeser Cohen and his brother-in-law, S. Rafael, were first to commercially show films in Portland; I.Leeser Cohen's house des. by E.M.Lazarus at 2343 N.W.Irving St.;I.Leeser Cohen survived by grandsons, Bates Solis Cohen and David Solis Cohen; and nephew, Leon M. Bernstein and niece,Judith S. Bernstein.

Alexander Bernstein (Isaac's 5th child) was a lawyer in Portland, OH & married into the Cohan family to Silva Solist Cohen

Family documents

Belle Bernstein Fink died in Providence, R. I., April 16, aged 74 years. She will be buried in Wiltwyck cemetery, Kingston, on arrival of funeral cortege from Providence at 2 a. m. Wednesday. Rabbi Blum of Temple Emanuel will conduct services at the grave. Mrs. Fink was born in Kingston, a daughter of Isaac and Henrietta Bernstein. She was a graduate of Kingston Academy and later was a teacher in School No. 8. She was married to David Fink 48 years ago and since that time had made her home in Providence. Besides her husband she is survived by one son, Adrian B. Fink, a resident of South Carolina, a sister, Flora Bernstein of New York city, and three brothers, Henry, Sam and Jacob Bernstein of Kingston.

Burial at Wiltwyck cemetery, Kingston NY for: Jacob, Grace, Harold Bernstein & Belle Bernstein & David Fink—memorial ID 159535654

Isaac, Henrietta, Flora & Henry Bernstein—Wiltwyck cemetery, Kingston, NY—plot block 42

Isaac Bernstein Family Documents

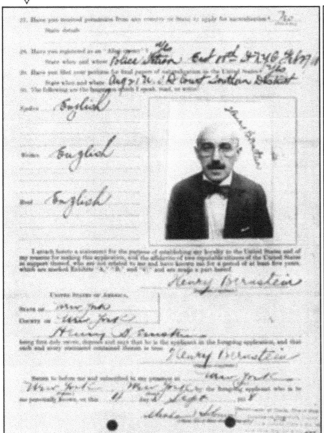

In re: Henry Bernstein   -2-

Brooklyn, N. Y., who told me that he had known Mr. Bernstein all his life; that Mr. Bernstein was born in Austria, came here when three years of age, and was a loyal American. Says that Bernstein can be trusted absolutely.

    Recommend that passport be issued. "

    Chief's telegram is attached to the New York office copy of this report.

             October 31st, 1918

    Since writing the above report, Mr. R. R. Jackson, A.P.L. has submitted the following:

    " Called on Henry Bernstein at his residence last evening, and had a lengthy conversation with him.   He stated that he was born in Russia, and came to this country when three years of age.   I found him to be thoroughly American and loyal in every respect.

    Am enclosing letter from Mr. Jos. P. Beranger's Secretary received from her yesterday. "

    The letter from Alice D. Fruh, Secretary to Mr. Joseph P. Beranger, of the West India Management & Construction Co., at 129 Front Street, New York City, reads as follows:

    "   I am in receipt of a reply to my letter to Mr. Beranger regarding Mr. Henry Bernstein. Mr. Beranger has known Mr. Bernstein for very nearly two years.   He is a steel erector of efficient ability, and were we in the field for a good, sober steel man we would not hesitate to employ him. Mr. Beranger has asked me to apologise to you for the delay in answering your request, as he is in a little country town with two mails a week. "

Henry Bernstein 1854-1935 (son of Isaac Bernstein) application for a passport when he went to Kingston, Jamaca to live for a time

Sam Bernstein

member of the board of trustees of the Ulster County Tuberculosis Hospital and took an active interest in the work of the hospital, devoting many hours of time to this work. He was a member of Lake Katrine Grange and Kingston Lodge, No. 10, F. & A.M., and that lodge will hold ritualistic services at the A. Carr & Son Funeral Home, 1 Pearl street, Sunday evening at 8 o'clock.

Surviving are his wife, Floretta Johnson Bernstein; a son Henry Bernstein of Phoenicia and a daughter, Martha Jean Morehouse of Croton-on-Hudson. Seven grandchildren also survive.

Friends may call at the A. Carr & Son Funeral Home, 1 Pearl street, Sunday from 2 to 4 and 7 to 9 p. m. where funeral services will be held Monday afternoon at 1 o'clock. Cremation will be at Gardner Earl, Troy, N. Y.

Sam Bernstein Jr. military registration WWI & WWII

Samuel Bernstein Jr. 1889-1956 (ran the family business after father Samuel Sr.)

Samuel Bernstein Sr. 1862-1935 (ran the family business after father Isaac)

Robert Bernstein: 1821–before 1857

Robert Bernstein was born in Gnesen, Prussia, in about 1821. He died prior to 1857.

Gustav Bernstein: 1824–before 1857

Gustav Bernstein was born in Gnesen, Prussia, in about 1824. He died prior to 1857.

Phillip Bernstein: 1825–1911

Phillip Bernstein is the next direct ancestor in our line. Information on him will be presented in the next section. Note that my family's direct ancestors' names are in red text to follow the genealogical line.

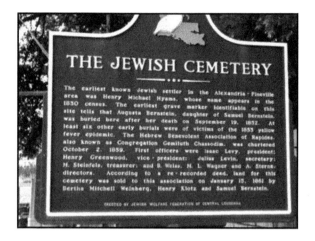

Augusta Bernstein, 1831–1865 (died of yellow fever)

Augusta Bernstein: 1831–1853

Just after 1850, Sam and Phillip Bernstein were joined in Louisiana by their sister, Augusta (Gussie) and brother, Morris. Unfortunately, in the fall of 1853, Augusta Bernstein took sick with yellow fever and died shortly after on September 17, 1853. The year 1853 went down in the history of Central Louisiana and Alexandria and vicinity as a very sad and tragic year. It was then that a severe plague of yellow fever struck. It was reputed to be the most malignant of all the yellow fever epidemics.

At that time, the small Jewish community of Alexandria faced a dilemma, for they had no cemetery for Jewish burial. Thirty Jews from Alexandria contributed thirty-four dollars each to purchase the land and organized the Hebrew Benevolent Society. Immediately, Samuel Bernstein, Abraham Mitchell, and Henry Klotz arranged the purchase of a parcel of ground in Pineville, which was to become the Jewish Cemetery for $100. Augusta's brother, Phillip Bernstein, named one of his children after his sister in 1865, but unfortunately that child only lived to 1867. [5]

> *NOTE: Augusta Bernstein has been erroneously identified as Samuel and Charlotte Bernstein's daughter in some published information. This error is repeated on the plaque marking the Jewish Cemetery in Pineville. The tombstone marking Augusta Bernstein's grave indicates that she was in fact twenty-two years old at the time of her death. In an oral history passed down through the Bernstein family (which was transcribed in about 1935 from Nettie Bernstein's memories), it states that* Augusta, daughter of Julius and Bertha Bernstein, *also died of yellow fever in 1867.*

> **Marker text**: *The earliest known Jewish settler in the Alexandria-Pineville area was Henry Michael Hyams, whose name appears in the 1830 census. The earliest grave marker identifiable on this site tells that* **Augusta Bernstein,** *daughter of Samuel Bernstein, was buried here after her death on September 19, 1852. At least six other early burials were of victims of the 1853 yellow fever epidemic. The Hebrew Benevolent Association of Rapides, also known as Congregation Gemiluth Chassodim, was chartered October 2, 1859. First officers were Isaac Levy, president; Henry Greenwood, vice-president; Julius Levin, secretary; M. Steinfels, treasurer; and B. Weiss, M. L. Wagner, and A. Sterne, directors. According to a re-recorded deed, land for this cemetery was sold to this association on January 15, 1861, by Bertha Mitchell Weinberg,* **Henry Klotz, and Samuel Bernstein.**

Morris Bernstein: 1834–1918

Morris (Maurice) Bernstein was born in Gnesen, Prussia, in October of 1834. In 1849–1850, he emigrated to the United States of America, along with his older sister, Augusta. Soon after arriving in America, they traveled to Alexandria, Louisiana, where they were reunited with their older siblings. It's believed that Morris lived with Samuel and Charlotte Bernstein initially and worked as a clerk in their store.

Morris Bernstein, 1834–1918

In 1852, after his older brothers, Samuel and Phillip, built their store at the crossroads that were to become the town of Winnfield, Morris moved to the new store and stayed with Phillip. For the next four years, Morris worked at the Winnfield store. In 1856, Samuel saw the opportunity to purchase property, including a store and warehouse, at the Red River port in Montgomery, Louisiana. Morris moved with Sam to Montgomery and served as a clerk and bookkeeper.

The capture of New Orleans by federal forces on April 25, 1862, brought the war home to many Louisianans. On May 7, 1862, Morris enlisted in the Confederate Army. He joined Company K. of the 28th Louisiana Regiment at Monroe, for which he was paid the customary $50.00 bounty. This was a new regiment, made up of ten companies, for a total of 902 men, many of whom were from Winn Parish. The regimental commanders were Colonel Henry Gray, Lieutenant Colonels William Walker and Isaac W. Melton, and Major Thomas W. Pool. The leader of Company K was Captain Darling P. Morris Bernstein's enlistment was for three years. From his enlistment documents, we learn that he had blue eyes, dark hair, a dark complexion, and was five-foot-three-inches tall. His height may seem short by today's standards; however, for his times he was probably just below the average. [6]

The Civil War and Winn Parish, 1861–1865...

(Article from The Southern Sentinel newspaper, Winnfield, LA)

The Civil War presented new problems to the Winn Parish Police Jury. The state had requested each parish to form "Home Guard" units and to form rifle companies to send into battle. Several parish leaders formed rifle companies of ninety men. The home guard units were to be under the supervision of the parish sheriff. The rifle companies did not have rifles, gun powder, rifle balls, uniforms, food or medical supplies. The families of the soldiers were left without financial support to provide food, clothing or shelter. The Police Jury voted to issue $5,000 worth of bonds to support the military effort and to provide for the families who in many cases were left destitute. They also did it to furnish ammunition for companies that had been organized for the protection of the parish against invasion or insurrection.

Winn Parish had five rifle companies of 90 men in the Confederate Army. Many others joined companies from adjoining parishes. More than 700 parish men were in uniform. The total population of the parish at that time was 4,600. Several Winn Parish residents joined the army from the North (The Yankees). One family had sons fighting on each side. There were also many Winn Parish men who refused the orders to report for duty with the Confederate Army. Some had joined groups resisting the war effort. Some were raiding homes and farms belonging to soldiers serving their country. Many men stayed in the woods during the day and returned to their homes at night. Only 16% of the Winn Parish men had joined the army. The Confederate Army saw the necessity of sending troops into the area to round up the deserters, draft dodgers, trouble makers and robbers.

William Walker, Winn Parish Sheriff from 1856 to 1861 took leave of his job in 1861 to join the Confederate Army. He left David McBride in charge of the sheriff office during his military leave. Col. Walker would never return to the sheriff's office as he was killed leading the 28th Louisiana Regiment in the battle of Mansfield.

Many Winn Parish men joining the Confederate Army in 1861 went to Montgomery and caught a riverboat to New Orleans. When they arrived in New Orleans they were issued uniforms to wear. The soldiers put their personal clothing and possessions in bags of boxes and put them on the freight and passenger ship going to Shreveport. The volunteers from Winn Parish put all their bundles in one box addressed to the care of S. Bernstein, merchant of Montgomery. The material was shipped to Samuel Bernstein's warehouse. This is where the trouble began! Samuel was charging exorbitant prices to some families who came to claim their husband's or son's possessions on a shipment that cost $3 to $4 for the whole lot. He threatened to burn or throw the baggage into the river unless the claims of 25¢ were paid. A public meeting was called and Samuel was chastened, his conduct called unpatriotic and ordered to deliver the soldier's possessions without fee or reward.

Treason in Winn Parish

Seventy-two Winn Parish residents signed a resolution (act of treason during war time) asking General U.S. Grand, the Commander of the Federal "Yankee" Troops, to intercede on their behalf and provide protection. They indicated they did not believe in the Confederate Government and the cause for which they were fighting. They wanted to be in good favor with the general in case the South lost the war. [7]

American Civil War 1861-1865

Morris Bernstein: Confederate Veteran

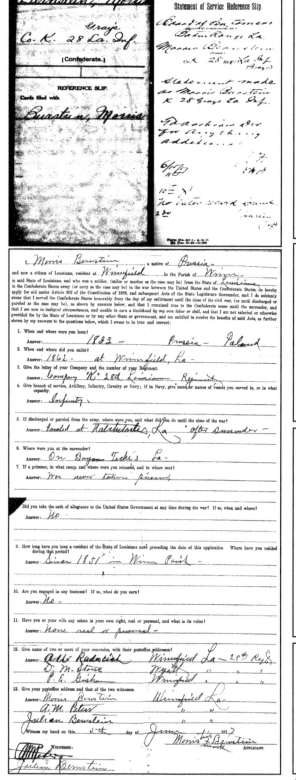

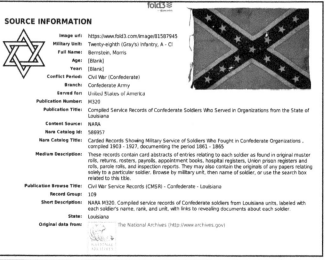

Winn Parish, Louisiana
Confederate Veterans

1/ William Murphy
2/ Robert C. Jones
3/ Mike W. Long
4/ Joseph Smith
5/ A.R. Butler
6/ John J. Dickerson
7/ William F. Shumake
8/ **Morris Bernstein**
9/ **Phillip Bernstein**
10/ Joseph M. Plunkett

11/ J. Matt McCain
12/ John G. Teagle
13/ Dr. Spencer M. Smith
14/ Jesse Womack
15/ David F. Dunn
16/ James D. Long
17/ George W. Story
18/ George A. Kelly
19/ Will A. Strong

CB CB CB

After the war, Morris is believed to have returned to Montgomery, Louisiana. He presumably took over the operation of Samuel Bernstein's store and warehouse after Sam and Charlotte moved to New Orleans in 1866. However, according to the history of the Bernsteins as dictated by Phillip's daughter, Nettie, Phillip moved to Montgomery in 1866, and Morris took over the Winnfield store. In the 1860 census, Morris is living with Samuel and working as a clerk in Montgomery, where they had constructed a store and trading center. Documentation shows that Morris returned to Winnfield in 1869 and bought Phillip Bernstein's store in Winnfield. It was then that he began the operation of what was to become known as "Uncle Morris's Corner."

Winnfield was still quite a small community at that time. Winn Parish offered opportunity to those willing to work hard in the local sawmills, rock quarry, or salt mine. There was never a real farm or plantation type economy in place. As such, it was seen to be a very tolerant community, with everyone working side by side. All indications are that the Bernsteins were well liked and accepted in the community. Evidence of this is the fact that Morris was accepted into the Eastern Star Masonic Lodge No. 151 on July 12, 1873. It requires unanimous consent from members for someone to enter a lodge. Morris went on to serve as treasurer of the lodge for over forty years. On December 14, 1907, he was made a "life Member," which is quite an honor.

For almost fifty years, Morris Bernstein operated the store on the corner of 10l East Main St. He tore down the wood frame structure and constructed the first brick store building in Winnfield. His property taxes in 1887 were $36.90. This may not sound like much, but by comparison, five hundred acres of land was taxed at about $6.00–$10.00. He paid one of the highest taxes in all of Winn Parish. For many years he operated his store as a credit store, but in 1900, he went on a cash basis. In 1910, his stock was valued at $8,000 (abt. $272,000 in today's purchase power), and he had a monthly payroll of $200.00.

M. Bernstein.

The subject of this article is one that is familiar to every old citizen of the parish and to every visitor for the past fifty-five years. When traveling in any section of the country, and it becomes known that you are from Winnfield one of the first questions you are asked "how is Uncle Morris Bernstein?" and they all have a pleasant recollection of him as is evidenced by the inquiry made about him.

Uncle Morris came to Winnfield in 1852 and has lived here continuously since that time except a short time that he lived at Trenton, and when the call for troops was made in 1862 he volunteered his services and became a member of Company K 28 Louisiana Volunteer Infantry, in which command he served until the close of hostilities, when he returned to Winnfield and commenced business again.

He is one of the public spirited men of the town. When he is shown that an enterprise is for the general welfare of the town he gives liberally. There is no church organization of any denomination not, only in Winnfield but anywhere in the parish, that can say they were ever turned away by him when applied to for assistance, but he has contributed liberally to every cause. In his acts of charity he has carried out the Biblical admonition, to not let his left hand know what his right hand was doing.

Uncle Morris is a friend to every one and every one is his friend, He has never married and his life's devotion has been to his brothers and their families. He is never so happy as when he is making some one else happy.

* * *

Bernstein's Store...

(*Article from The Southern Sentinel newspaper, Winnfield, LA*)

The first store constructed on the future site of Winnfield and the parish Seat of Justice was the Bernstein Store. The question is often asked, "How did the Bernstein brothers, Phillip and Samuel know where to construct their famous store?" Dennis Mackie, surveyor and police juryman from Ward 4, had surveyed several parish boundaries and quite often would hold a barbecue sponsored by some well-to-do individuals and would make the participants aware of opportunities for investment in future land developments.

According to the 1860 Winn Parish Census a surveyor living at Wheeling was listed as the individual having the greatest financial wealth in Winn Parish. The relatively rich Bernstein brothers were living 50 miles from the future Winnfield site. Phillip and Samuel Bernstein were in the merchandising business on Little River. The Bernsteins also had a profitable business in buying pine knots and shipping them down river to New Orleans where the pine was processed into illuminating gas to light the city of New Orleans.

In 1852 Phillip and Samuel Bernstein came to Winn Parish and purchased a plot of ground at the intersection of two roads. The Bernstein brothers started to construct a store building at this famous intersection after two weeks of hard work. They sent for their 18 year old younger brother Morris to come to Winn Parish and help with the construction of the store.

Dennis Mackie and his surveying crew were busy selecting the site for the Seat of Justice in Winn Parish. Ben Teddlie had a farm across the road from the Bernstein Store where the courthouse was built in 1886. Mackie convinced Ben Teddlie that his property was needed for the Seat of Justice for Winn Parish. Teddlie sold the property for $75.

The surveying crew laid out the wide streets starting at the Bernstein store, running east, west, north and south from that point. The entire block across from the Bernstein's Store was reserved for the future courthouse.

In 1856 Samuel saw the opportunity to purchase property, including a store and warehouse at the Red River port in Montgomery. Morris and Phillip had some family problems and Morris went with Samuel to serve as clerk and bookkeeper in Montgomery. Phillip remained in Winnfield to operate the store. Morris returned to Winnfield in 1864 and purchased the store from Phillip when he was 35 years of age. Morris did not establish the store, but was very successful and later tore down the old frame store building to build the first brick store building on the spot. He was a mason and a very charitable man always helping others. Morris never married and in 1910 reported to the local Southern Sentinel newspaper that his stock value was $8,000 and his payroll per month was $200. Morris operated the store for many years as a credit store, but in 1900 he went on a cash basis. He operated the store until his death. In 1986 the building was still standing on the corner of 101 Main Street in the heart of Winnfield. [8]

WINNFIELD, LOUISIANA, FRIDAY, AUGUST 19, 1910.

The Oldest Store	**M. BERNSTEIN** ESTABLISHED 1852.	The Newest Prices

Special All the Week from Now until Aug. 27

(Prices will Change. Watch this Space.)

Special Offer on Sugar this week

18 lbs. Standard Granulated Sugar............ $1.
18 lbs. Y. C. Sugar .... $1.

New Syrup, qt. cans,........15c	50lb. Pure Yellow Chops $1.40
New Syrup, ½-gal. cans....30c	50lb. Wheat Bran _____ $1.40
New Syrup, 1 gal. cans....50c	30lb. Shorts ____ '____ $1.50
Highest Patent Flour bbl $7.25	Cottonseed Meal, 100 lb sk $1.75
High Pat. Flour 24lb sack 90c	100lb. C. S. Hulls _____ 75c
Cream Meal 24lb Sack... 55c	No.2 White Oats 4 bu sck $2.50
Pearl Meal 24lb Sack... 50c	
Wrapped Bacon............ 18c	Choice Alfalfa Hay bale 80c
Bacon, Extra Clear Sides 17c	Choice Prarie Hay bale 45c
Dry Salt Bellies _____ 16c	Choice Timothy Hay... 85c
Gold Brand Hams......... 21c	Choice Bermuda Hay... 70c

Special on *Cottolene*

2 lb. Bucket - - 30c
4 lb. Bucket - - 60c
10 lb. Bucket - $1.40

ORDERS FILLED PROMPTLY

Phone 13.   Terms: Spot Cash

101 Main Street today

Although Morris Bernstein never married, he is said to have had an illegitimate child by Pernecia Almarinda Allen. The boy's name was Prindo (or Prendo) Allen. He was born in Winn Parish on March 19, 1876. Pernecia was twenty-one years old at the time, so it isn't known why they would not have married. Prindo Allen married Mary L. Elizabeth Mercer on April 20, 1893, and they had seven children. Their first, Dewey Clifton Allen, was elected Mayor of Winnfield on June 28, 1950. His wife, Mary Allen, succeeded him when elected on June 9, 1960, and served as Mayor of Winnfield until 1970.

In 1912, Morris Bernstein was assaulted during a robbery of his store and was left an invalid for the remainder of his life. At four o'clock in the afternoon of June 6, 1918, Morris Bernstein died. His body was transported on the Louisiana and Arkansas Railroad to Alexandria, where he was interred in the Jewish Cemetery at Pineville. Rabbi L. J. Rothstein officiated. The body had been accompanied by about twelve members of the Winnfield Masonic Lodge, who were joined in Pineville by members of Oliver Lodge.

In his will, he left his entire estate to Rosalia Bernstein, widow of his brother Phillip. Morris Bernstein was said to have been a very charitable man and a very honorable businessman.

Signs in Winnfield, LA honoring the Bernsteins

CB CB CB

Morris Bernstein 1834-1918 - Store

The Comrade, Winnfield, Souvenir Series

M. Bernstein's Store, the first brick store in Winnfield, La.

Old Grocery Store Was Emporium that Attracted Buyers

Boss Simms established the first store in Winnfield, at what date, is not known, and Phillip Bernstein the second immediately after. The Bernstein store first under the management of Phillip and then that of his brother Morris continued to do business in this city for many years.

There are few stores operating today as they were in the early days. With the streamline interiors, glass show windows, and a cash register that does everything but deliver merchandise and collect past due bills, the wonder is how they did it in the old days.

The smell of the general merchandise store that handled everything from hair nets to harness is unforgettable. It was a mixture of everything which combined to produce one of the most pleasant aromas imaginable. It was an out-side world smell that made a customer feel that he had really gone somewhere.

The rows of flour barrels and the white and brown sugar in sacks and barrels. The vinegar barrel always dripping at the spout. The cured meat in a screened box and the old pot-belled stove tobacco stained. Bolts of calico cloth and gingham checks and the old cracker barrel into whose stock sneaked many pilfering fingers. Side combs, horse collars, buggy whips in a fancy stand—It was all on one floor a grand dress rehearsal for all to see and enjoy. But last and not least, the sack of hard candy for the kids when the bill was settled.

Store employee—Ike Gans

Uncle Sam's Corner Store at various years—from oldest to more recent times
101 East Main Street, Winnfield, Louisiana. The bottom one is the brick building constructed by Morris Bernstein as it currently appears. Picture was taken in March 1997.

- 39 -

Morris Bernstein 1834-1918 - Store

*Morris Bernstein
1834-1918*

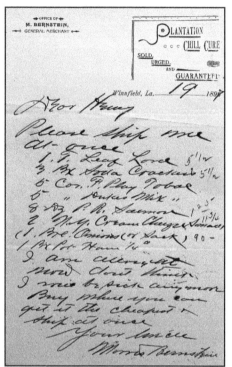

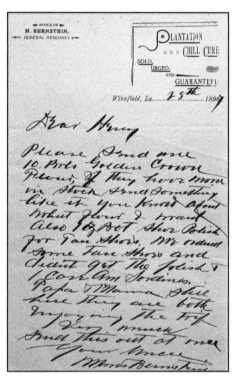

Letters from Morris Bernstein to Henry Sr. & Julius Bernstein to Henry Sr. regarding the store. Dated 1897

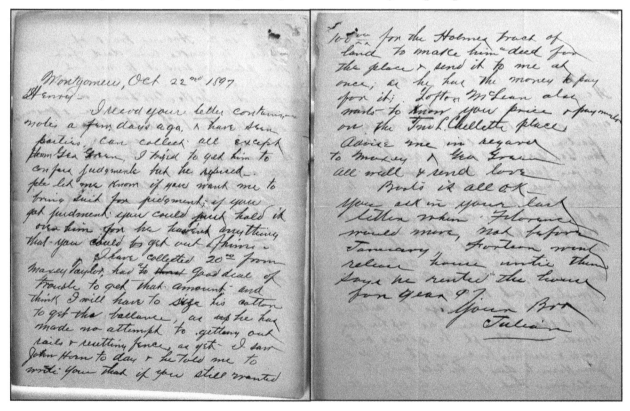

Life in Winn Parish, LA in the 1800s

3 photos of lumber camp in Winn Parish, Louisiana—showing logging operation— the company store & men working on the railway.
Image courtesy of Toby Stewart & Sally Stewart from the estate of Myrta Reace Stewart Persons

Early Transportation

Salt Mining Winnfield, Louisiana

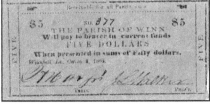

Winn Parish currency 1863

Rebecca Bernstein: 1836–before 1857

Rebecca Bernstein was born in Gnesen, Prussia in about 1836. She died prior to 1857.

Adolph Bernstein: 1838–before 1857

Adolph Bernstein was born in Gnesen, Prussia in about 1838. He died prior to 1857.

Mary Bernstein: 1840–unknown

Mary Bernstein was born in Gnesen, Prussia in about 1840. In 1857, she immigrated to the United States of America with her parents. She settled in Kingston, New York, where she married a Mr. Pinner. This is all that is currently known of Ma ry.

Joseph B. Bernstein: 1841–1910

Joseph Bernstein was born in Gnesen, Prussia on August 20, 1841. In 1857, he immigrated to the United States of America with his parents and sister, Mary. By 1860, he was living with his brother Samuel and working for him as a clerk in the Bernstein clothier store.

Although relatively new to Louisiana, perhaps looking for adventure, or perhaps because he strongly believed in the Confederate cause, Joseph joined the Confederate Army soon after the beginning of the war. On August 18, 1861, he enlisted as a private in Company C of the 12th Louisiana Regiment at Montgomery, Louisiana. He entered his training soon after at Camp Moore with the other 703 men in the regiment. The regimental commander was Colonel Thomas M. Scott. The captain of Company C, also known as the Southern Sentinels, was John A. Dixon.

In February 1865, the regiment went to North Carolina and joined the army of General Joseph Johnson again. The men fought their last battle at Bentonville on March 19, 1865. On April 26, the regiment surrendered at Greensboro. Due to the poor quality of the copies of his parole record, it's not clear where Joseph Bernstein was released after the war or when. My best guess is Augusta, Georgia, on May 20, 1865. After the war, it is believed he returned to Montgomery, Louisiana.

On November 27, 1873, he married Jenette (Budislofski) Marks. She was the younger sister of Rosalia, wife of Phillip Bernstein. Joseph became a postmaster for Bonner Jackson, Louisiana in 1879, Lincoln, Louisiana in 1881, and Shreveport, Louisiana in 1900. Then the couple moved to Coushatta, in Red River Parish, Louisiana. Joseph was alive on April 19, 1910 for the census and listed as a hotel proprietor. He must have died after April 1910 and Jenette died August 23, 1912 in Coushatta, Red River, Louisiana.

CB CB CB

Now back to Phillip Bernstein and his family. Phillip is my great-great-grandfather, and the remainder of this section on the Bernsteins follows my direct decedents.

Phillip Bernstein: 1825–1911

Phillip Bernstein was born April 10, 1825, in Gnesen (Gnienzo in modern Poland), province of Posen, Prussian Poland. Records back in Gnesen were all lost after WWII when Hitler razed the old Jewish cemetery and built a warehouse on the land. To my knowledge, no Jews ever re-established themselves in Gnesen after this. The Jews of Gnesen came to Poland mainly from the west and the southwest, and from the very beginning were of Ashkenazi culture. Ashkenazim is one of the two major groupings of Jews, who originated in Eastern Europe and descended from ancient Hebrews. They were settlers who established communities along the Rhine River in Western Germany and in Northern France dating to the Middle Ages. All of our information from those earlier times is from family stories passed down to each generation, and history books.

According to oral history from Phillip's daughter Nettie in 1950, Phillip ran away from home at eleven years old. He made his way to Birmingham, England, where he lived for about seven years and learned to speak English. The date of his immigration to the United States of America is between 1841, 1843, or 1845, as noted on various census records, obituaries, and family stories. In the 1910 Louisiana census, Phillip stated that he immigrated to the US in 1843, which would have made him eighteen years old when he left England. He sailed to the US on the ship *Shenandoah*, landing in New York, where he apparently worked as a tailor mending clothes for the theatre. Tailoring seems to be a family trade, and I wonder what the family did back in Gnesen, Posen while their father Julius was at war. The earliest US census I have found was November 18, 1850 and has Phillip at twenty-five is living with his older brother, Samuel, who is thirty-three, his wife, Charlotte, and brother Isaac, twenty-one. Both Phillip and Isaac are listed working as peddlers for Samuel's trading post, carrying various wares in packs on their backs as they traveled the dusty roads of Louisiana. They learned the highways and byways of the country, gaining the good will and support of all classes of citizens. They were known to be honest, industrious men of fair and equitable business dealings, truly pioneer merchants of the time.

In 1852 he and his brother Samuel learned of the establishment of a new parish in Louisiana, with the seat proposed to be at the intersection of North-South Military Road and Buckskin Road, which became Montgomery, Grant Parish in the future. The brothers built a general store there in three months and waited the two years until the town was officially established on April 14, 1854. Phillip continued to travel with his wares while they waited for the town to be established. Phillip became a naturalized citizen of the US in 1855. The original naturalization certificate is on one of the previous photo pages.

Phillip Bernstein 1827-1911

Phillip is buried in Jewish Cemetery in Pineville, Rapids Parish, Louisiana in row 15.

Phillip was a member of the Masons

PHILIP BERNSTEIN.

The Colfax Chronicle of July 15th, has the following to say about Philip Bernstein, who died in Winnfield, La., on Friday, July 7th, 1911 at 9 a. m., and whose remains were brought to Alexandria for interment, notice of which appeared in Town Talk at the time.

"He was born in Pose, Germany in 1827, and died in the 85th year of his age.

"He came to the United States in 1841, and in the early forties settled in Alexandria. He moved to Winnfield when Winn parish was organized, and remained there until 1866, when he moved to Montgomery, La., and lived there until the early eighties, when he moved across Red river into Natchitoches parish, where he engaged in farming and merchandising until 1900 when he returned to Winnfield, where he remained to his death, having been in poor health for the last ten years of his life.

"He was the last charter member living of Eastern Star Lodge F. & A. M. No. 151; was also a charter member of I. O. B. B. Lodge at Natchitoches, and was in connection with both orders at the time of his death. He was in the Confederate army and made a gallant soldier. He is survived by his wife, two brothers and six children. His children are, Hon. Henry Bernstein, of the Monroe law firm of Hudson, Potts & Bernstein. Arnold Bernstein and Mrs. Kaliska who also live at Monroe, Julian, Rudolph and Miss Nettie Bernstein who

Phillip & Rosalia Bernstein ~ Family Chart

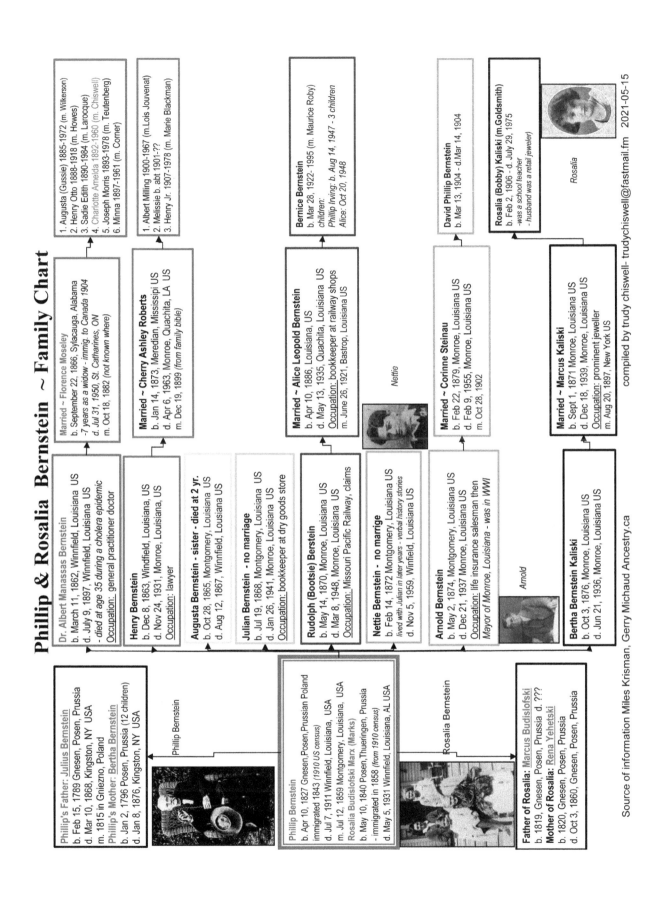

Dr. Albert Manassas Bernstein
b. March 11, 1862, Winnfield, Louisiana US
d. July 9, 1897, Winnfield, Louisiana US
- died at age 35 during a cholera epidemic
Occupation: general practitioner doctor

Married ~ Florence Moseley
b. September 22, 1866, Sylacauga, Alabama
-7 years as a widow - immig. to Canada 1904
d. Jul 31, 1950, St. Catharines, ON
m. Oct 18, 1882 *(not known where)*

1. Augusta (Gussie) 1885-1972 (m. Wilkerson)
2. Henry Otto 1888-1918 (m. Howes)
3. Sadie Edith 1890-1984 (m. Larocque)
4. Charlotte Amelda 1892-1960 (m. Chiswell)
5. Joseph Morris 1893-1978 (m. Teutenberg)
6. Minna 1897-1961 (m. Comer)

Henry Bernstein
b. Dec 8, 1863, Windfield, Louisiana, US
d. Nov 24, 1931, Monroe, Louisiana, US
Occupation: lawyer

Married ~ Cherry Ashley Roberts
b. Jan 14, 1873, Meredian, Mississipi US
d. Apr 6, 1963, Monroe, Quachita, LA US
m. Dec 19, 1899 *(from family bible)*

1. Albert Milling 1900-1967 (m.Lois Jouvenat)
2. Melissie b. abt 1901-??
3. Henry Jr. 1907-1978 (m. Marie Blackman)

Augusta Bernstein - sister - died at 2 yr.
b. Oct 28, 1865, Montgomery, Louisiana US
d. Aug 12, 1867, Winnfield, Louisiana US

Julian Bernstein - no marriage
b. Jul 19, 1868, Montgomery, Louisiana US
d. Jan 26, 1941, Monroe, Louisiana US
Occupation: bookkeeper at dry goods store

Rudolph (Bootsie) Berstein
b. May 14, 1870, Monroe, Louisiana US
d. Mar 8, 1948, Monroe, Louisiana US
Occupation: Missouri Pacific Railway, claims

Married ~ Alice Leopold Bernstein
b. Apr 10, 1886, Louisiana, US
d. May 13, 1935, Quachita, Louisiana US
Occupation: bookkeeper at railway shops
m. June 26, 1921, Bastrop, Louisiana US

Bernice Bernstein
b. Mar 28, 1922- 1995 (m. Maurice Roby)
children:
Phillip Irving: b. Aug 14, 1947 - 3 children
Alice: Oct 20, 1948

Nettie

Nettie Bernstein - no marrige
b. Feb 14, 1872 Montgomery, Louisiana US
lived with Julian in later years - verbal history stories
d. Nov 5, 1959, Winfield, Louisiana US

Arnold Bernstein
b. May 2, 1874, Montgomery, Louisiana US
d. Dec 21, 1937 Monroe, Louisiana US
Occupation: life insurance salesman then
Mayor of Monroe, Louisiana - was in WWI

Married ~ Corinne Steinau
b. Feb 22, 1879, Monroe, Louisiana US
d. Feb 9, 1955, Monroe, Louisiana US
m. Oct 28, 1902

David Phillip Bernstein
b. Mar 13, 1904 - d.Mar 14, 1904

Arnold

Bertha Bernstein Kaliski
b. Oct 3, 1876, Monroe, Louisiana US
d. Jun 21, 1936, Monroe, Louisiana US

Married ~ Marcus Kaliski
b. Sept 1, 1871 Monroe, Louisiana US
d. Dec 18, 1939, Monroe, Louisiana US
Occupation: prominent jeweller
m. Aug 20, 1897, New York US

Rosalia (Bobby) Kaliski (m.Goldsmith)
b. Feb 2, 1906 - d. July 29, 1975
-was a school teacher
- husband was a retail jeweler

Rosalia

Phillip's Father: Julius Bernstein
b. Feb 15, 1789 Gnesen, Posen, Prussia
d. Mar 10, 1868, Kingston, NY USA
m. 1815 in Gniezno, Poland
Phillip's Mother: Bertha Bernstein
b. Jan 2, 1796 Posen, Prussia (12 children)
d. Jan 8, 1876, Kingston, NY USA

Phillip Bernstein

Phillip Bernstein
b. Apr 10, 1827 Gnesen,Posen,Prussian Poland
immigrated 1843 *(1910 US census)*
d. Jul 7, 1911 Winnfield, Louisiana, USA
m. Jul 12, 1859 Montgomery, Louisiana, USA
Rosalia Budislofski Marx (Marks)
b. May 10, 1840 Posen,Thueringen, Prussia
- immigrated in 1858 *(from 1910 census)*
d. May 5, 1931 Winnfield, Louisiana, AL USA

Rosalia Bernstein

Father of Rosalia: Marcus Budislofski
b. 1819, Gnesen, Posen, Prussia d. ???
Mother of Rosalia: Rena Yehetski
b. 1820, Gnesen, Posen, Prussia
d. Oct 3, 1860, Gnesen, Posen, Prussia

trudychiswell@fastmail.fm   2021-05-15

compiled by trudy chiswell-

Source of information Miles Krisman, Gerry Michaud Ancestry.ca

Phillip Bernstein 1827-1911

STATE OF LOUISIANA,
PARISH OF Winn

On this 18 day of November 1915, personally appeared before me PK Abel, Clerk of the District Court, within and for said Parish and State, Mrs. Rosalia Bernstein aged 74 years, a resident of the town of Winnfield Parish of Winn and State of Louisiana, who being duly sworn according to law, declares that she is the widow of Phillip Bernstein, who entered the service of the Confederate States during the civil war under the name of Phillip Bernstein at Winnfield La ~~on the~~ about ~~day of~~ Jan 1863 in Co "G" 28th La Regiment of Infantry (Here state rank, company and regiment, or vessel) as a private (Hardy's Company, Gray's Regiment) from the State of Louisiana that he served honorably until fall or Winter of 1863 at which time he secured permit from Col. Gray to become Deputy Sheriff under John Brown the then sheriff of Winn Parish La ~~and that he remained true to the Confederate States, until the surrender, at which time he was~~ having been appointed Deputy Sheriff as aforesaid by Governor Allen of Louisiana

that she was married to the said soldier under the name of Rosalia Marx on the 17th day of July 1859, by David Hardy J.P. at Montgomery La that she has not married again, and that she is now in indigent circumstances and unable to earn a livelihood by her own labor or skill, that she is not married or otherwise provided for by the State of Louisiana or by any other State or Government; that her said husband died on the 8th day of July 1911; at Winnfield La that she has resided in the State of Louisiana for 1857 years next preceding the date of this application, and that she claims the aid and benefit of Article 303 of the Constitution of 1898 and subsequent Acts of the Legislature of the State thereunder as is further shown by her answers to the following questions which she swears to be true and correct:

1. Under what circumstances did your husband die?
   Answer: Nervous prostration from complications & old age.
2. Where is he buried?
   Answer: Pineville La.
3. What are your means of support?
   Answer: None.
4. What is the value of your property, real and personal, if any?
   Answer: Community interest in house & lot in Winnfield assessed $215
5. Have you conveyed property to any one in the past few years?
   Answer: No.
6. If any. How much and to whom conveyed?
   Answer: Conveyed none.
7. Give your postoffice address and that of your two witnesses.
   Answer: Rosalia Bernstein Winnfield La.

Witness my hand on this 18th day of Nov 1915

Witness: R Bernstein — Rosalie Bernstein, Applicant.

Minna Marx

Also personally appeared Rudolph Bernstein residing at Winnfield La and Minna Marx residing at Winnfield La. persons whom I certify to be respectable and entitled to credit, and who being by me duly sworn, say that they were present and saw Mrs. Rosalia Bernstein, the claimant, sign her name to the foregoing declaration, and that they verily believe that the facts and declaration of said claimant are true and correct, that their acquaintance with her for 40 years and 15 years respectively, justify them in making this statement, and that she is the identical person she represents herself to be, and that they have no interest in the prosecution of this claim.

R. Bernstein
Minna Marx

Sworn to and subscribed before me on this, the 18 of Nov 1915, and I hereby certify that the contents of the above declaration were fully made known and explained to applicant and witnesses, and that I have no interest, direct or indirect, in the prosecution of this claim.

PK Abel
Clerk 5th Dist, Clerk of Court.

14882

Parish of Winn

No. 3-15-16

WIDOW'S APPLICATION FOR PENSION

THE BOARD RESERVES THE RIGHT TO CALL FOR ADDITIONAL TESTIMONY

Mrs. Rosalie Bernstein
Widow of Phillip Bernstein
Company and Regiment G 28th La Inf
P.O. Winnfield La
Filed Dec 1st 1915
Allowed
Quarterly Allowance, $
Pension Allowed from
Rejected 3/15/16 no record

President

O.F. Brian, Secretary.
Board of Pension Commissioners.

Cause of Death of Widow's Husband?
Nervous Prostration
When Did He Die?
8th July 1911
Where?
At Winnfield La
Date of Granting Pension?
Monthly Amount?
Date of Application?
Nov 18th 1915

TO SAVE DELAY, APPLICANTS SHOULD FURNISH ALL DOCUMENTARY EVIDENCE THEY MAY POSSESS, AND SWORN STATEMENTS OF COMRADES OF THEIR HUSBANDS WHEN OBTAINABLE.

All applications should be addressed to the Secretary of Pension Commissioners, at Baton Rouge.

Blanks will be furnished by the Secretary on request.

Regular meetings of the Board, second Tuesdays in March, June, September and December.

—OFFICE OF—

COMMISSIONER OF LOUISIANA MILITARY RECORDS.

Send the names and postoffice of any Confederate living you may know.

All persons who have rolls of Companies are requested to loan or donate them towards helping to complete this important work.

By Authority of Act No. 156, Legislature of Louisiana.
Approved July 2nd. 1908.

882
File

~~T. W. CASTLEMAN,~~ COMMISSIONER. A.B.Booth,
No. ~~604 CANAL-LA. BANK BLDG.~~ 216 N. O. Courthouse.

NEW ORLEANS, LA., Dec. 27, 1915. ~~190~~

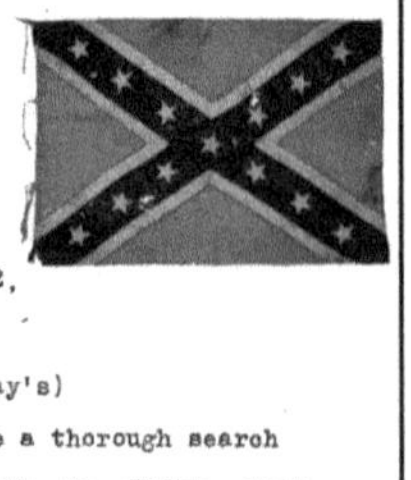

Col. E. F. Brian, Sec.,
Pension Board,
Baton Rouge, La.

Dear Sir:--

Yours of the 1st. inst., #14882,

PHILLIP BERNSTEIN.
Co.G. 28th. La. Infty. (Gray's)

Beg to advise that we have made a thorough search of the rolls, in our possession, of the 28th. La. Infty., both Gray's and Thomas' but fail to find his name of record therein.

Yours truly,

A.B.Booth
Commissioner, La. Military Records.

Winnfield La March 15th 1864

P. D. Hardy Sec of State
Shreveport

Dr Sir Some time ago I sent up a return ~~asking for Phillip Bernstein~~ to be Commissioned as Coroner of the Parish of Winn. But the Commission has not Come & thinking the uncertainty of the mail to be the reason I write this and ask you to Send the Commission by the bearer of this Mr B. was duly elected at our general election in Nov last. Your attention will much oblige

J. C. Brown
Sheriff of Winn

STATE OF LOUISIANA,
PARISH OF RAPIDES, } ss.

Be it Remembered,

That on the _____ day of _____ January _____ in the year of our Lord one thousand eight hundred and _____ fifty-five _____ Philip Bernstein _____ late of the Kingdom of Bavaria _____ appeared in the District _____ Court of

at present of the Parish of Rapides, State of Louisiana _____ [the said Court being a Court of Record having a Common Law Jurisdiction, and a Clerk and Seal] and applied to the said Court to be admitted to become a Citizen of the United States of America, pursuant to the directions of the Act of Congress of the United States of America, entitled "An Act to establish an uniform Rule of Naturalization, and to repeal the Acts heretofore passed on that subject; and also to an Act entitled an Act in addition to an Act entitled an Act to establish an uniform Rule of Naturalization, and to repeal the Acts heretofore passed on that subject; and also to an Act entitled "An Act supplementary to the Acts heretofore passed on the subject of an uniform Rule of Naturalization, passed 30th day of July 1813," and to the Act relative to Evidence in cases of Naturalization, passed 22d March, 1816, and an Act, in further addition to an Act, to establish an uniform Rule of Naturalization, and to repeal the Acts heretofore passed on that subject, passed May 26th, 1824;" and an Act entitled "An Act to amend the Acts concerning Naturalization, passed May 24th, 1828; And the said _____ Philip Bernstein _____ having thereupon produced to the Court such evidence, made such declaration and renunciation, and taken such oaths as are by the said act required _____ he submitted, and he was

Philip Bernstein

THEREUPON it was ordered by the said Court, that the said _____ accordingly admitted by the Court, a CITIZEN OF THE UNITED STATES OF AMERICA.

IN TESTIMONY WHEREOF, the Seal of the said Court is hereunto affixed, this _____ 4th _____ day of _____ January _____ in the year of our Lord one thousand eight hundred and _____ fifty-five _____ and in the _____ 79th _____ year of the Independence of the United States

PER CURIAM.

_____ CLERK.

The store was known for many years as "Uncle Morris' Corner" and did business that became widely known from Mississippi to Texas. As late as 1900, Morris Bernstein continued to bring merchandise by steamboats on the Red River. Morris was Phillip's younger brother and built up the business to a large, prosperous operation while remaining single all his life.

On July 12, 1859, Phillip married Rosalia (Budislofski) Marks of Gnesen, Posen, Prussia. She was born Budislofski, but European names were so difficult for the English government official to pronounce in the United States that when they reached New York, she took her father's given name, Marks, before she married Phillip. This also might have been a throwback to before Prussia made the Jews take surnames. Before surnames were brought into law in 1820 in Prussia, Rosalia would have been referred to as Rosalia daughter of Marks, or Rosalia ben Marks. In 1857, Rosalia landed in New York with her soon to be father and mother-in-law, Julius and Bertha Bernstein. Shortly after, she continued her journey, sailing to New Orleans, where she was met by Mr. Goldsmith, a family friend. Mr. Goldsmith accompanied her to Sam and Charlotte's home in Montgomery. After their marriage, the couple spent their honeymoon at Sam's plantation across the river in Natchitoches Parish. It was said by Phillip's sister Nettie that the couple wore out a set of Mohair furniture and drank baskets of champagne while they were at Samuel's home in Montgomery. It was at that time that Samuel and Charlotte went to New York to visit his parents.

The 1860 census has Phillip at thirty-two years old and listed as a merchant living in Winnfield, Louisiana with Rosalia, who was nineteen years old. Their first child was Albert Manassas, my great-grandfather, born March 11, 1862. Albert's middle name was to commemorate the first major victorious Confederate Battle of Manassas in 1861.

The original Bernstein home was located at what is currently 404 West Main Street, Winnfield, Louisiana. Currently there is a new home with a business called Sunshine Cleaners there on the corner of Main and John Street. One street back is Bernstein Street, which dead ends into the back of what was the Bernstein property.

Both Morris and Phillip Bernstein were privates in the Confederate Army. Morris joined the army in 1861, staying engaged in the war until the end in 1865, but was not a prisoner of war. According to the widow's pension application of Phillip's wife, Rosalia, Phillip joined in January 1863, and in the winter of the same year he had been appointed by Governor Allen of Louisiana to the position of Deputy Sherriff in Winnfield under Sherriff John Brown. Phillip was granted dismissal from the army and returned to Winnfield. It's not known if he did become a Deputy Sherriff, but I found another document from March 15, 1864, from Sherriff John Brown asking that Phillip Bernstein be conscripted as Coroner of Winn Parish.

Winnfield, LA   March 15th, 1864
P.D. Handy Sec of State
Shreveport

Dear Sirs

Some time ago I sent up a return asking for Phillip Bernstein to be conscripted as a Coroner of the Parish of Winn. But the conscription has not come and thinking the uncertainty of the mail to be the reason. I write this and ask you to send the commission by the bearer of this. Mr. B was duly elected at our general election in Nov last. Your attention will much oblige.

John C. Brown
Sheriff of Winn

Rosalia's petition for widow's pension was denied because they couldn't find Phillip's military record, but he must have been in the war or the old Confederate Veterans of Winn Parish would never have allowed him in the following photo of 1906.

Pioneer Life in Winn Parish, Louisiana

In the 1850 census, there were at least twenty-four Jewish inhabitants of Winn Parish, Louisiana. Many more arrived, as is evident from the 1860 census. The Jews approximately represented about .5 percent of the population of Rapides Parish and 1.8 percent of the city of Alexandria. Yet it must be remembered that at any one particular time, there was a transient population particularity of Jewish peddlers, who plied their ware in and around the parish in the early days. Phillip and Morris Bernstein were two of them initially until the stores were established and they became prominent citizens and merchants of Winnfield and Monroe. The 1860 census of Winn Parish reveals the population growth and the density of the population. It shows Phillip Bernstein as a merchant at thirty-two, and his brother Morris as a merchant at eighteen years old. There is also an Abram Bernstein, a twenty-five-year-old barber, and I wonder if he was a cousin of Phillip and Morris.

When Winn Parish was created in 1852 from portions of other parishes, there were provisions made for a parish seat. The parish seat settled upon is within two or three miles of the exact center of the parish. The location was a high rolling, well drained land, which was heavily timbered with the virgin forest of pine and oak. A military road made by General Jackson in 1812 ran through the middle. It was surveyed and plotted. The name of Winnfield was finally agreed on for the town.

The year 1853 went down in the history of Central Louisiana and Alexandria and vicinity as a very sad and tragic year. It was then that a severe plague of yellow fever struck. It was reputed to be the most malignant of all the yellow fever epidemics. At that time, the small Jewish community of Alexandria faced a dilemma, for they had no cemetery for Jewish burial. Thirty Jews from Alexandria contributed $34 each to purchase the land and organized the Hebrew Benevolent Society. Immediately, Samuel Bernstein, Abraham Mitchell, and Henry Klotz arranged the purchase of a parcel of ground in Pineville, which was to become the Jewish Cemetery, for $100. Samuel Bernstein lost his sister Augusta to the yellow fever epidemic, and she was the first to be buried in the new Jewish cemetery. The cemetery was turned over to the Hebrew Benevolent Society of Congregation Gemiluth Chassodim in 1861. Many of the records of the Jews in Winn Parish were lost when the courthouse was destroyed by fire.

Smoke Pots for Mosquitoes

Pioneer families living in early Winn Parish had never seen or heard of screen doors or windows for their homes. Insects, including mosquitoes, bugs, and flies, were a nuisance. Families had to rely of smoke pots to help control the problem. Before retiring for the night, the mother or one of the children would prepare a smoke pot and smoke the rooms to the point you could hardly breathe. Quite often the pots of clay had sand in the bottom to prevent fire. The smoking materials used varied from rags, bark, and green leaves to dried cow manure. Quite often sulphur was sprinkled on the smoldering material. By the 1900s several new ideas had been developed to combat the stinging, biting, and harmful pests. [9]

℃℈ ℃℈ ℃℈

Winnfield was still quite a small community at that time. Winn Parish offered opportunity to those willing to work hard in the local sawmills, rock quarry, or salt mine. There was never a real farm or plantation type economy in place. As such, it was seen to be a very tolerant community, with everyone working side by side. All indications are that the Bernsteins were well liked and accepted in the community. Evidence of this is the fact that, Morris was accepted into the Eastern Star Masonic Lodge, No. 151, on July 12, 1873. It requires unanimous consent from members for someone to enter a lodge. He went on to serve as treasurer of the lodge for over forty years. On December 14, 1907, he was made a "life Member," which is quite an honor.

In 1866, Phillip and the family moved to Montgomery after the Civil War. In the 1870 US census, the family was living in Montgomery, Parish of Grant, Louisiana with four children plus Phillip's brothers: Samuel with his wife, Charlotte, brother Isaac, and Rosalia's sister Jenette Marks. Three years later, Jenette married Phillip's younger brother, Joseph, on November 27, 1873. In the census, Phillip is forty-five and listed as a dry goods merchant, with the value of his real estate at $200 and the value of his personal estate at $15,000. Both Samuel and Isaac are listed as clerks in a store, probably Phillip and Morris's store. It was stated by his daughter Nettie that her father bought some silver bullion on the levee in New Orleans, and a man named Levy made them into spoons and forks, which Nettie used daily into her old age.

There is a family story that Phillip purchased slaves, and one of his slaves was named Jennie (Jenny) Katz. Phillip sired a child with Jennie before he was married named Alexander Bernstein, born in 1853.

NOTE: See more about Jennie at the end of this section on the Bernsteins.

The family continued to live in the Parish of Grant, Louisiana in the 1880 census with six children. Albert Manassas, the oldest, is already out of the house living and working with his uncle Morris in Winnfield, Louisiana as a clerk in the store. This is before Albert goes to New Orleans Medical College, where he graduated.

After many years of life as a successful dry goods merchant, Phillip lived a semi-retired life on his little plantation on Red River, just across the river from Montgomery, in Natchitoches Parish. He had been one of the successful merchants of Winnfield and returned there in 1901, where he remained until his death at eighty-five years of age on July 7, 1911. His remains were brought to Alexandria for burial in the Jewish Cemetery in Pineville, Rapids Parish, Louisiana, row 15. Rabbi I. Heinberg of Monroe, assisted by members of Oliver Lodge (Masons) of Alexandria, officiated the funeral.

At his death, Phillip was a charter member of Eastern Star Lodge No 151, Ancient Free and Accepted Masons at Winnfield from 1860. Both he and his brother Morris were staunch supporters of the cause of the Democratic Party and were public-spirited citizens.

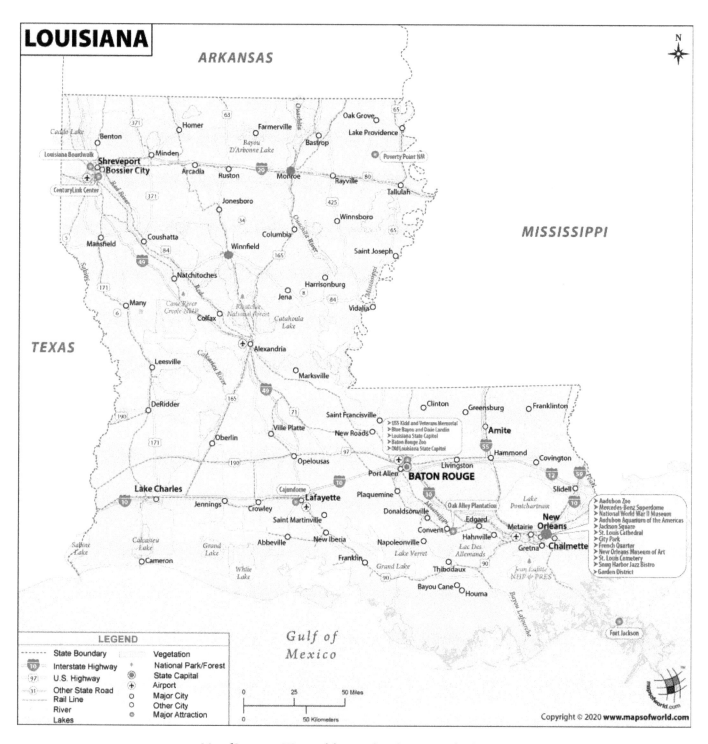

Map of Louisiana, USA – red dots are where the Bernstein families lived

Life in Winnfield, LA in 1800s

The roads Phillip Bernstein travelled

Main Street, Winnfield, Louisiana—Image courtesy of the LSU Libraries Special Collection

Winnfield, LA - Main Street—N. of Square, Runing W.

Baptist Tabernacle, Winnfield, LA

COURT STREET, LOOKING WEST, WINNFIELD, LA.

MAIN STREET, LOOKING EAST, WINNFIELD, LA.

Rosalia Budislofski: 1840–1931

Rosalia Marks

Young Rosalia Marks

Phillip married Rosalia (Budislofski) Marks, born May 10, 1840, in Gnesen, Posen, Prussia. Her parents were Marcus Budislofski and Rena Yehetski of Gnesen, Posen, Prussia. In 1857, Rosalia was fifteen years old when she accompanied one of her aunts from Prussia and her soon to be father and mother-in-law, Julius and Bertha Bernstein. Rosalia didn't know her future husband before coming to the US. Julius and Bertha Bernstein stayed in New York, and Rosalia carried on to Louisiana to marry Phillip in Montgomery, Louisiana on July 12, 1859 The family story is that when Rosalia came to the US, she couldn't speak English, and whoever was registering her put her father's name of Marks down as her last name, since Budislofski was hard to pronounce. Leaving New York at sixteen years old, Rosalia continued on another sailing ship to New Orleans, Louisiana where she was met by Mr. Goldsmith and taken to Sam Bernstein's home, where she later married Phillip.

By the reports, Rosalia was a kind soul, and when her oldest son, Albert Manassas, had married my great-grandmother, Florence Moseley, she welcomed her new daughter-in-law into the family by teaching her to sew her new husband's shirts. Florence's mother had died when she was very young, so she hadn't had a mother's influence in her life during her growing up years.

After Phillip died in 1911, the census shows that Rosalia continued to live in their West Court Street home along with her daughter, Nettie, and son, Julian, both living at home and looking after their mother. Nettie and Julian never married. Julian was a real estate broker and bookkeeper in a dry goods store, which was probably the family store Phillip and his brother Morris started in Winnfield. Also living with the family in Winfield was Rosalia's sister Minna, who Minna Corner, one of Albert Manassas's children, was named after.

Rosalia (Budislofski/Marks) Bernstein, 1840–1931 in rocker with Charlotte Amelda (Bernstein) Chiswell in the back left (my grandmother).
The other two people are not known, but the woman may be Minna Budislofski, Rosalia's sister.

With the support of her devoted family, Rosalia spent her retirement in comfort. Over the many years in the United States, she had become fluent in the English language, and it is said she spoke with no trace of a foreign accent. She had always been deeply interested in the politics of the state as well as the nation. In fact, Winn Parish has long been a hotbed of Louisiana politics. Governor Huey Long was a Democrat from Winnfield and a contemporary of the Bernstein's. Rosalia had always enjoyed reading, as well as spending time outdoors.

Rosalia's sister, Minna Budislofski Marks, never married and lived with her sister in Winnfield, where it is believed she died on March 8, 1942.

On May 5, 1931, Rosalia (Budislofski/Marks) Bernstein passed away and was interred in the Monroe Jewish Cemetery. Her sister, Minna (Budislofski) Marks, who died March 8, 1942, and her son, Julian Bernstein, who died January 26, 1941, are both buried beside her. Rosalia's obituary in the Winnfield News American newspaper shows how she was valued in her community and gives insight into her life.

The Winnfield News American newspaper

May 8, 1931

Death Claims Mrs. Rosalia Bernstein Tuesday Afternoon

Beloved Winn Ph. Citizen Laid to Rest in Jewish Cemetery in Monroe

Winnfield News America

May 8, 1931

Mrs. Rosalia Bernstein, age 91, one of Winnfield's most beloved and distinguished citizens died at 3:50 o'clock Tuesday afternoon at her home on Main Street. Mrs. Bernstein would have celebrated her 91st birthday next Sunday, "Mother's Day" at which celebration her sons and daughters were to be present. She had been in failing health for several months but displayed a remarkable vigor of mind and body until her death.

Since 1857 Mrs. Bernstein has been a resident of Winn Parish and because of her interest in affairs in general as well as her sweet and amiable disposition she was well known throughout this section.

Mrs. Bernstein, whose maiden name was Rosalia Marks, was born in Germany, May 10, 1842. When a young lady 17 years old she came to America with her parents who settled in Winn Parish when she married Philip Bernstein, a prominent Red River planter. For many years she resided in Montgomery and later moving back to Winnfield.

Her deep interest in educational and social developments in the state never wavered during her long and useful life. Being the mother of some of the most popular citizens of North Louisiana Mrs. Bernstein manifested a keen interest in affairs of state and the careers of her children.

Funeral services conducted by the three local pastors, Rev. Alwin Stokes, of the Presbyterian Church, Rev. A. H. Cullen, of the Baptist Church, and Rev. C. C. Weir of the Methodist Church were held at the home Wednesday morning at nine o'clock just before the funeral cortege left for Monroe, where final services were held at three o'clock in the afternoon and interment made in the Jewish Cemetery with Rabbi F. K. Hirsch officiating.

As a tribute of respect all business houses in Winnfield were closed Wednesday morning for one hour during the brief home services, while the offices in the city hall of Monroe were closed all day and the city schools closing at noon.

An escort of four policemen, and four firemen of Monroe accompanied the body to Monroe Wednesday morning, and the cortege was met in West Monroe by another escort of motor-cycle police who led the funeral procession through the two cities to the cemetery. The bell in the Monroe City Hall tolled as the cortege entered West Monroe and continued the requiem until the cemetery was reached.

Mrs. Bernstein is survived by her sons Henry Bernstein, Rudolph Bernstein and Arnold Bernstein of Monroe, Julian of Winnfield, and her daughters Mrs. Marcus Kaliski of Monroe, and Miss Nettie Bernstein of Winnfield. A sister, Miss Minnie Marks of Winnfield, and a brother, Sam Marx of New Orleans, also survive, besides a large number of grandchildren.

Among the friends attending the funeral in Monroe were Mack L. Branch, J. R. Heard, J. L. Tugwell, J. W. Teddlie, Alvin S. Hahn, of Winnfield and Mr. and Mrs. H. B. Johnson and Mr. and Mrs. H. R. Moore of Shreveport.

CB CB CB

Rosalia and Phillip Bernstein's children

1. Albert Manassas: (March 11, 1862–July 9, 1897) became a doctor and married Florence Moseley (my great-grandparents)

2. Henry: (December 8, 1863–November 24, 1931) became a lawyer and married Cherry Ashley Roberts

3. Augusta: (October 28, 1865–August 12, 1867) died young at two years old

4. Julian: (July 19, 1868–January 26, 1941) never married, became a bookkeeper in a dry goods store

5. Rudolph (Bootsie): (May 14, 1870–March 8, 1948) became a claims officer for the Missouri Pacific Railway and married Alice Leopold

6. Nettie: (February 14, 1872–November 5, 1959) never married, lived with her mother and Julian in the family home till her death

7. Isaac: (abt 1873–March 17, 1921) never married, became a salesman in a dry goods store

8. Arnold: (May 2, 1874–December 21, 1937) became an acclaimed Mayor of Monroe, Louisiana for twenty years, married Corinne Steinau

9. Bertha: (October 3, 1876–June 21, 1936) an elementary schoolteacher, married Marcus Kaliski, a leading jeweler in Monroe, Louisiana

10. There is also a story of a slave, Jennie Katz Bernstein, who had a child, Alexander Bernstein, by Phillip.

Albert Manassas Bernstein: 1862–1897

Albert Manassas Bernstein is the next direct ancestor in my family line. Full information on him is in the next section.

Henry Bernstein: 1863–1931

Henry Bernstein, 1863–1931

Henry Bernstein was born on December 8, 1863, Winnfield, Louisiana. As a child, the school year was spent in New Orleans with his brother, Albert Manassas, at Uncle Sam and Aunt Charlotte's home. There he attended Jackson Boys' Academy and later attended Tulane University, graduating in 1886 with a Bachelor of Laws degree.

The Law Department of Tulane University was organized in 1847. The degree of Bachelor of Laws, granted by the University, authorized the person upon whom it was conferred to practice law in the state of Louisiana. Among its graduates were some of the most respected lawyers in the state.

The annual course of instruction commenced in mid-November and was completed the following May. Unlike most other states of the Union, Louisianan justice was based on Roman Civil Law. Therefore, in addition to the courses in the Law of Nature and Nations, Admiralty and Maritime Law, the Common Law, Equity and Constitutional Law, which were common curriculum in most law schools of the time, it was also necessary to study Civil Law in Louisiana. The fee for the course was fifty dollars. There were apparently no extra charges. Upon graduation, a public commencement was held. Henry Bernstein's commencement was held at the Grunewald Opera House on Saturday, May 15, 1886. William Preston Johnston, LL. D., President of the University, presented the degrees. There were fourteen students in the Class of 1886.

After graduation, Henry returned to Winnfield to begin his law practice. On December 4, 1890, he became the District Attorney for Winn Parish. Earlier that same year, he had been accepted into the Eastern Star Masonic Lodge No. 15 I., and on March 8, 1890, he had achieved his Master Mason Degree. On December 29, 1894, he was commissioned the Registrar of Voters for the Parish.

Cherry Ashley Roberts

Henry married quite late by the standards of his day. He was thirty-six years old when he married Cherry Ashley Roberts on December 19, 1899. It's not currently known where their wedding took place; however, about that time or shortly after, Henry and Cherry Bernstein moved to Monroe, Louisiana. Their first child, Albert Milling Bernstein, was born October 12, 1900, in Monroe. Their second child, Henry Bernstein Jr., was also born in Monroe, on October 31, 1906.

Shortly after going to Monroe, Henry became a member of the law firm Hudson, Potts, Bernstein & Scholars. This may have been the reason for the move. Monroe was much larger than Winnfield and therefore presented greater opportunities for a lawyer. One of the more prestigious clients he served as legal representative was the Missouri Pacific Railroad.

Later, both of his sons graduated from Tulane University with law degrees and joined the firm. Henry Bernstein continued to work with his sons until the time of his death on November 24, 1931. This was only six months after the death of his mother. He was interred in the Monroe Riverside Cemetery in Monroe, Louisiana. Cherry (Roberts) Bernstein died April 6, 1963 and was interred beside her husband.

Albert Milling Bernstein married Lois Jouvenat on November 21, 1925, and had a son, Henry III, on September 25, 1926, and a daughter named Cherry Louise (after her grandmother), born on December 20, 1929.

Henry Bernstein Family 1863-1931

Cherry Ashley Roberts

Cherry Ashley Roberts Bernstein 1873-1963 with baby Milling

Henry Bernstein Sr. as a young man 1863-1931

All the Men in the Family Were Lawyers

Milling Bernstein 1900-1967 son of Henry Sr.

Henry Bernstein Jr. 1907-1978 son of Henry Sr.

Henry Bernstein Sr. Monroe Homes

Henry Bernstein Sr. first home
on Jackson Street
Not sure who all the children
were on the front step, but it
gives us an look at the dress of
the day.

Henry Sr. & Cherry Bernstein home on Riverside Street, Monroe, Louisiana—across from the levee for Ouachita river

Henry Bernstein Sr. 1863-1931

DEATH CLAIMS WELL KNOWN LOCAL LAWYER

Henry Bernstein Sr., Brother of Mayor, Succumbs Suddenly

FUNERAL WEDNESDAY

Demise Removes One of Outstanding Members of Bar Ass'n

Henry Bernstein, member of the law firm of Hudson, Potts, Bernstein and Sholars, and brother of Mayor Arnold Bernstein of this city succumbed from a sudden stroke of apoplexy shortly after 7 o'clock this morning at his home, 1706 Riverside. While his health had been failing for the past few months, he had been able to attend to business several hours daily, hence his death came as a great shock to an unusually wide circle of friends.

Mr. Bernstein was born in Grant Parish on December 8, 1863. He was educated in the public schools, largely in Winn Parish, and later attended Soule College, New Orleans. After this he entered Tulane University where he was graduated with the class of 1886.

The same year, Mr. Bernstein was admitted to the State Bar Association, and began the practice of law in Winn Parish. In 1897 he removed to this city and became a member of the legal firm of Potts & Hudson as the present firm was then designated, Col. F. G. Hudson, Sr. and I. J. Potts being members of the firm at that time.

From the outset, the connection with this firm proved highly successful and

(Continued on Page Two)

DEATH CLAIMS H. BERNSTEIN

(Continued from Page One)

the company became one of the leading of its kind in North Louisiana. In 1914, Allan Sholars became a member of the firm which then was styled as at present, Hudson, Potts, Bernstein and Sholars.

During the last years of his life, Colonel Hudson was general attorney for Louisiana for the Missouri Pacific Railroad Company and at his death, Mr. Bernstein succeeded to this position which he maintained up to the time of his death.

Mr. Bernstein was married years ago to Miss Cherry Roberts of Winn Parish, who survives as do two sons, who are: Milling Bernstein and Henry Bernstein, Jr., both members of the same firm as was their father.

Mr. Bernstein also leaves several brothers and sisters. Mayor Arnold Bernstein of Monroe, is a brother, as is Rudolph Bernstein of Monroe, claim agent for the Missouri Pacific Railroad and Julian Bernstein of Winnfield. There are also two sisters who are Mrs. Marcus Kaliski of Monroe, and Miss Nettie Bernstein of Winnfield.

Mr. Bernstein was an honored member of the local bar association, of the Louisiana State Bar Association, and of the Fourth District Bar Association of the Fifth Judicial District.

He was a man of quiet demeanor and was not much of a club man in the general sense of the word. However, he was an active Mason for years and also was affiliated with the Knights of Pythias in which organization he held a number of official posts in years gone by. He was a member of the Elks Lodge and it was

Henry Bernstein Sr. 1863-1931

Louisiana State Bar Association

Mrs. Bernstein Dies Saturday; Rites Pending

Mrs. Cherry Roberts Bernstein, a longtime resident of Monroe, died at her home at 1706 Riverside Dr. Saturday night.

A native of Meridian, Miss., Mrs. Bernstein had resided here for the past 65 years. She was widow of the late Henry Bernstein Sr., a Monroe attorney.

Mrs. Bernstein was a member of First Methodist Church here.

Funeral services are incomplete, but will be under direction of Peters Funeral Home of Monroe.

Survivors include two sons, A. Milling and Henry Bernstein Jr., both of Monroe; a sister, Mrs. Ruby Roberts Steward of Monroe; a brother, Earl Roberts of Colfax, three grandchildren and five great-grandchildren.

"Milling" Bernstein Family 1900-1967

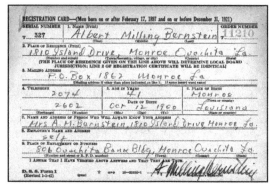

Albert "Milling" Bernstein 1900-1967

Lois Kilborne Jouvenat- Milling's wife

Lois Kilborne Jouvenat with Henry III

Lois Kilborne Jouvenat Bernstein 1905-1997

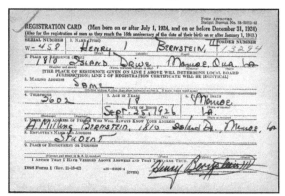

Albert Millings son Henry III
Milling's son &Henry Sr.'s grandson

Cherry Louise Bernstein
Milling's daughter &Henry Sr.'s granddaughter

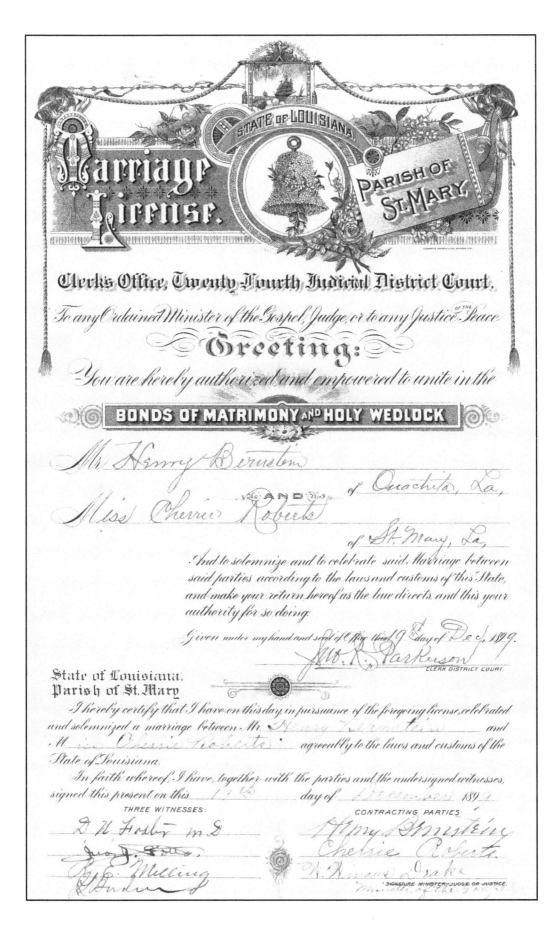

Augusta Bernstein: 1865–1867

Augusta Bernstein, 1865–1867

Augusta Bernstein was born October 28, 1865, in Winnfield, Louisiana. She was named after Phillip's sister, who had died twelve years earlier of yellow fever. This Augusta didn't live long and died August 12, 1867, at home in Winnfield, Louisiana, at just two years old.

CB CB CB

Julian Bernstein: 1868–1941

Julian Bernstein was born July 19, 1868, in Montgomery, Louisiana. He attended public school at Jackson Boys' Academy in New Orleans, living with his Uncle Samuel and Aunt Charlotte for a while. By 1886, he was working as a clerk for Norton's Cotton Buyers. Later he moved back to Winnfield and worked in his Uncle Morris's store until his uncle retired in 1900.

Julian never married. After his parents moved back to Winnfield in 1900, he presumably lived with them on West Court Street. After his father died in 1911, Julian managed his mother's estate, which included seven brick buildings in Winnfield. Later he was successfully engaged in general real estate business and is said to have had an authoritative knowledge of land values throughout that section of Louisiana. He had planned a new development of a family monument on "Uncle Morris's Corner." Possibly because of the Great Depression, his dream was never realized.

On January 26, 1941, Julian died and was buried beside his mother and Aunt Minna Marks in the Jewish Cemetery, Monroe, Louisiana.

ᘓ ᘓ ᘓ

Rudolph Bernstein: 1870–1948

Rudolph Bernstein was born May 14, 1870, in Montgomery, Louisiana. He was affectionately known as "Bootsie." On June 26, 1921, Rudolph married Alice Leopold, and one year later, the couple had a daughter named Bernice. The family lived in Monroe, where Rudolph was employed as an assistant claim agent for the Missouri Pacific Railroad. Before their marriage, Alice was listed on the 1920 census as a bookkeeper at a railway shop, so perhaps that's how they met. Bootsie was a familiar figure in Winnfield, where his family had been well known for many years. When he retired five years before his death, he was given a big party in the Virginia Hotel in Monroe.

Alice (Leopold) Bernstein died May 13, 1935, after a lingering illness. It was stated in the newspaper obituary that a large number of people paid their tribute to the local woman at her residence on 107 Texas Avenue in Monroe. Rabbi F.K. Hirsch of Temple B'Nai Israel conducted the service. The floral offerings were especially numerous and came from persons in varied walks of life. Alice was from an old and influential family of northeast Louisiana, the daughter of Mr. and Mrs. S.A. Leopold of Bastrop.

Rudolph's death on March 12, 1948, after a short stay in the Monroe hospital, was a shock to his many friends. The couple is interred in the Jewish Cemetery, Monroe, Ouachita Parish, Louisiana.

It's reported that Rudolph Bernstein also sired a Black boy by a slave named Rebecca Davis in 1893. Rebecca died in 1920, and Rudolph married Alice in 1921. More about the Black side of the Bernsteins at the end of the section.

Their daughter, Bernice, married Maurice Roby and had two children, Phillip and Alice, while living in Monroe, Louisiana. Phrose Raphael, now ninety-five and a friend of the family, grew up with Bernice. She remembers her friend's red hair and when she came to visit in Bastrop, Louisiana. Phrose has fond memories of when Bernice came to visit her grandparents Leopold and play marbles with her under the raised house. Apparently, Bernice was a bit of a tomboy and always won all the marbles. "Mom loved hunting and fishing and was definitely a unique woman. She was a great mother and very involved in the community and school," recounts her son, Phillip. Bernice's son, Phillip Irving Roby, had three children and was a helicopter pilot in the Vietnam on medical evacuation. He now lives in California and remembers growing up in Winn, Louisiana. Bernice and Maurice had two children, Phillip and Alice.

1. Phillip Irvin Roby: b. Aug 14, 1947
2. Alice Roby: b. Oct 20, 1948

Rudolph Bernstein 1870-1948

Alice (Leopold) Bernstein

Alice & Rudolph (Boots) Bernstein

Rudolph with Phillip Roby as baby & Nettie in back

Alice & Rudolph (Boots) Bernstein

Rudolph was a claims agent for the
Missouri Pacific Railroad

The Monroe News-Star.
Tuesday, May 14, 1935

MRS. BERNSTEIN'S
FUNERAL IS HELD.

Large Number Of Persons Pay Final Tribute
To Local Woman.

A large number of persons paid final tribute to Mrs. Rudolph Bernstein, 48, at her residence, 107 Texas avenue, at 5 p.m. Tuesday, when her funeral was conducted by Rabbi F. K. Hirsch of Temple B'Nai Israel. Mrs. Bernstein died at her home late Monday afternoon after a lingering illness. Interment was made in the Jewish cemetery. The floral offerings were especially numerous and came from persons in varied walks of life.

Pallbearers were J. R. Ludlum, John Morris, George Beckman and George Khourt, all of Bastrop, and Edgar Florsheim, Henry Haas, Ed Strong, and L. J. Hart, all of Monroe. Mrs. Bernstein was from an old and influential family of northeast Louisiana, the daughter of Mr. and Mrs. S. A. Leopold of Bastrop. Her maiden name was Miss Alice Leopold.

Surviving are Mrs. Bernstein's husband, Rudolph Bernstein, claim agent of the Missouri Pacific railroad and brother of Mayor Arnold Bernstein; one daughter Miss Bernice Bernstein; her parents, a sister Miss Stella Leopold, of Bastrop and a brother, Alvin Leopold of Bastrop.

Rudolph Bernstein's Family

$2.00 PER ANNUM

Bernice Bernstein Weds Maurice A. Roby November 18

(Monroe Morning World.)

A wedding characterized by charming simplicity and one that claimed the interest of friends here and throughout the state took place November 18th in the home of Mrs. Arnold Bernstein, when hr nece, Miss Bernice Bernstein, daughter of Mr. Rudolph Bernstein and the late Mrs. Alice Leopold Bernstein, became the bride of Maurice A Roby, son of Mr. and Mrs. Harry Roby, of Newellton, La.

The ceremony, witnessed by the members of the family and a few intimate friends, took place at 2:30 o'clock in the afternoon with Rabbi F. Hirsch, officiating.

The reception suite was candlelit and banked with beautiful white crysanthemums and white carnations. White crysanthemums also banked the improvised al.ar before which the ceremony was performed.

The bride's attendant, Mrs. Herman Moyse of Washington, D. C., wore a lovely lime green, light weight wool suit with accessories of a darker shade of green and corsage of camellias.

The bridegroom was attended by his father.

The bride, given in marriage by her father, wore a beautiful three-piece ensemble of azure blue, an Adele Simpson model. A small, close fitting hat of blue and accessoies of blue were worn. A corsage of orchids added a note of distinction.

An informal reception was held following the ceremony with Mrs. Bernstein wearing a handsome dinner dress of dubonnet and green embroidered in iridescent beads and a corsage of pink camellias. Mrs. Roby, the bridegroom's mother, assisting in receiving, wore a black crepe dinner model with corsage of white camellias.

The bride's table in the dining room, appointed in silver, was overlaid with handsome lace and centrally adorned with the three-tiered wedding cake. Plaques of white carnations were placed at the four corners and at either end of the table were placed silver candelabra supporting white tapers.

A supper course was served from a spacious buffet centrally adorned with a silver basket overflowing with white bride's roses and white carnations. Toasts to the bride and bridegroom were drunk in champagne.

Following the honeymoon in New Orleans Mr. and Mrs. Roby will be at home in Newellton.

The bride is a graduate of the Neville High School Northeast Junior College and the Louisiana State University. Mr. Roby is a graduate of the Newellton High School and Louisiana Tech. He was with the armed forces in Italy for four years.

Phillip Roby & father at his Bar mitzvah

Bernice & Maurice Roby with children: Alice & Phillip

NEWS from the Services

1968

Philip I. Roby, son of Mr. and Mrs. Maurice A. Roby, Newellton, La., prepares to fire the M-60 machine gun during Army small arms training.

A student at Northeast Louisiana State College in Monroe, Cadet Roby is attending Army Reserve Officers' Training Corps summer camp. The course began June 14 at Ft. Sill, Oklahoma.

During the encampment, he is receiving six weeks of training in physical conditioning and other military subjects.

Upon successful completion of summer camp and graduation from College, he is eligible to be commissioned as a second lieutenant in the U. S. Army.

Cadet Roby is a member of Zeta Beta Tau fraternity and a 1965 graduate of Newellton High School.

Fishing - One of Bernice's passion growing up was to go fishing on the Bayou.

SERIAL NUMBER 1217	1. NAME (Print) Maurice Aaron Roby		ORDER NUMBER 3153
2. ADDRESS (Print) 351 West Madison St., Bastrop, Morehouse, Louisiana			
3. TELEPHONE 405	4. AGE IN YEARS 24 DATE OF BIRTH Oct. 19 1915	5. PLACE OF BIRTH N. Y., N. Y	6. COUNTRY OF CITIZENSHIP U. S. A.
7. NAME OF PERSON WHO WILL ALWAYS KNOW YOUR ADDRESS Mrs. Bessie Aaron Roby			8. RELATIONSHIP OF THAT PERSON Mother
9. ADDRESS OF THAT PERSON Newellton, Tensas, Louisiana			
10. EMPLOYER'S NAME Seligmans, Inc.,			
11. PLACE OF EMPLOYMENT OR BUSINESS 125 So. Franklin St., Bastrop, Morehouse, Louisiana			
I AFFIRM THAT I HAVE VERIFIED ABOVE ANSWERS AND THAT THEY ARE TRUE.			
REGISTRATION CARD D. S. S. Form 1			Maurice Aaron Roby

Nettie Bernstein "Tutter" ~ June 1953 in her home in Winnfield, LA

Nettie Bernstein "Tutter": 1872–1959

Nettie Bernstein

Nettie Bernstein was born February 14, 1872, in Montgomery, Louisiana. She never married and lived with her parents throughout her life. Nettie taught music at Zion and also taught school for a period of time, making $80 which she gave to her father to have the cotton picked. She boarded with Oscar Allen's grandmother, teaching Oscar at school and riding him to school on her horse every morning.

After her father death in 1911, Nettie shared duties of administering her mother's estate with her brother. Julian. She was affectionately known at "Tutter" to the family and was author of the only known written family history from that time. While her work was somewhat brief, it has provided many glimpses into the past, and much of her work was incorporated into the research Miles Krisman did in the late 1900s and in this book.

After her mother's death, during the Great Depression, the family home was refinanced in order to provide Nettie with a home until her own death on November 5, 1959. She was interred in the Jewish Cemetery in Monroe, Louisiana. The following is the original letter sent to my grandmother, Charlotte Bernstein Chiswell, asking for sign off of for the refinancing of the house for Tutter.

LAW OFFICES
HUDSON, POTTS & BERNSTEIN
OUACHITA NATIONAL BANK BUILDING
MONROE, LOUISIANA

JOHN J POTTS
F. O. HUDSON, JR
MURRAY HUDSON
A. MILLING BERNSTEIN
HENRY BERNSTEIN, JR.

May 17th, 1934

Mrs. Charlotte Cheswell,
Conniston, Canada

Dear Charlotte:

We have been trying to refinance the Bernstein home
in Winnfield, and mortgage the same to the Home Owners
Loan Corporation, in order that Tutter may use it for
the rest of her life.

In order to do this, it will be necessary that we
get quitclaims from all of the heirs.

We are taking this up with them and I am sure that
you have received a letter from Tutter about the
matter.

All of them at the present time have consented to
this procedure and we have heard from them all with
the exception of you, Albert and Louise, whom
we will undoubtedly hear from within the next few
days.

We will appreciate more than we can tell you, your
signing these papers for us, because this is the
only way we know of that the home can be refinanced,
and saved for Tutter.

It will probably be several weeks before the papers
can be drawn up and forwarded to you, however, I will
do so just as soon as we have secured all the
necessary data and information, and I will forward
them to you for your signature at that time.

Trusting that you are well and happy, I remain

Your cousin,

72.

Henry Bernstein jr.

Letter from Henry Bernstein to my grandmother, Charlotte Chiswell

l is the Home Paper of Winn Parish People.

SIANA, FRIDAY, NOVEMBER 22, 1907.

WILLIAM WALKER CHAPTER MEETS

Touching Resolutions Adopted and Reception Marks an Enjoyable Occasion.

Wm. Walker Chapter, Daughters of the Confederacy, held their regular meeting last Wednesday afternoon with Miss Mina Marks at the residence of Mr. M. Bernstein, a confederate veteran. There was a very large attendance of the members, attesting the deep interest felt in the organization.

The routine business of the Chapter was transacted. The first was the adoption of resolutions of sympathy on the death of Mr. J. T. Wallace, for the sister Daughters, Mrs. Cas Moss and Mrs. E. E. Kidd, daughters of the deceased copies to be furnished to The Sentinel and Comrade, also to each of the above ladies and spread upon the minutes of the William Walker deapter.

A committe composed of Edna Brian, Gamble, Hattie Jones and Anna Machen presented the following:

"Again has the silver cord been loosened and the golden bowl been broken and the pitcher been broken at the fountain." The Death Angel has entered a happy home and taken the guide and stay. A kind, indulgent father, a devoted husband, a true and noble man has passed to his reward. Inasmuch as in the transition of Mr. James T. Wallace, our sisters, Mrs. Cae Moss and Mrs. Earl Kidd have lost a kind and loving father, Be it ordained: First, that we, the Daughters

of the Confederacy, extend to them our heartfelt sympathy in this hour of trial.

Second, That we feel a sense of our own loss in that a noble-hearted friend and neighbor has passed away.

Third, That we commend them to Jesus, the only Comforter, who wipes all tears away. He alone can heal their wounded and broken hearts."

Respectfully.
EDNA BRIAN GAMBLE,
HATTIE JONES,
ANNA MACHEM.
Committee.

After the adoption of these resolutions Miss Mina Marks invited her guests to the dining room to partake of a most profuse and elegant repast consisting of turkey and all the accessories that usually surround that most splendid domestic fowl, comprising cake, coffee, nuts, etc.

The dining room was beautifully decorated with ferns and other pot plants to add their charm of beauty to the occasion. Miss Mena Marks made a most gracious hostess and was assisted in pleasantly entertaining her guests by her sister, Mrs. P. Bernstein and Neice, Miss Nettie Bernstein. This pleasant conclusion of a very interesting meeting of the Chapter was highly appreciated and enjoyed by the members.

Mr. M. Bernstein, a Confederate veteran felt honored by and greatly enjoyed the meeting at his residence and evinced the greatest interest in the proceedings, as he is somewhat of an invalid.

* * *

Smith-Grisham Drug Co. has a full line of tablets, pens, pencils and school books. s27tf

The Jewish Cemetery in Monroe, Louisiana

Cotton pickers in the early years. Nettie gave money to her father to help pay for the cotton pickers.

Arnold Bernstein: 1874–1937

Arnold Bernstein was born on May 2, 1874, in Montgomery, Louisiana. He was educated in the Louisiana Public School system and then attended the Soule Business College in New Orleans, perhaps staying with his Uncle Samuel and Aunt Charlotte.

In 1896 at the age of twenty- two, he moved to Monroe, Louisiana. On October 22, 1902, he married Corinne Steinau. They made their home at 819 North Second Street and became the local representative for the New York Life Insurance Company in 1905. He was with the company for six years and then represented Equitable Life for twelve years. He was distinguished as one of the very successful insurance men of the state. Arnold and Corinne were unable to have any more children after their one child died one day after being born. Both Arnold and Corinne were community-minded people and actively involved in their community.

Since early manhood, Arnold had taken a keen interest in civic affairs and acted on his conviction that citizens should discharge their civic responsibilities to the full. His first public office was serving as alderman for four years. In 1919, he was elected as Mayor of Monroe, Louisiana and served continually until his death in 1937. His re-election in 1927 was an unopposed campaign, a feat that had not been accomplished before in Monroe.

During his terms in office, Monroe experienced its greatest industrial and commercial growth to that time, due in part to Arnold Bernstein's foresight and sound management. He wasn't a man that everyone always agreed with, however. He saw a growing city with a need for recreational areas. His contemporaries saw the action he took to meet that need as "Bernstein's folly." The "folly" was 147 acres of land located between Sandifer and Thomas streets, east of Wilson Street. He purchased the land for the city on September 17, 1928, for $42,642. People called it a folly because it was in a low area of the city and populated with nothing but a bunch of pine oak trees. Today it has become a local tourist attraction know as Louisiana Purchase Gardens and Zoo. Not only did his "park folly" turn into a Monroe attraction, but during the Great Depression, a public garden was maintained there to grown vegetables like potatoes, beans, cabbage, and other greens to be distributed to local families in need. A nursery for the cultivation of trees and shrubs was also established, as well as a lagoon in the 1930s.

Arnold was a community-minded individual. He was an active member of the B'nai Israel Synagogue in Monroe as well as the Chamber of Commerce, the Rotary Club, and the Lotus Club. He also served as chairman of the executive committee of the Tensas Basin Flood Control Association and assisted with federal flood control programs in north-eastern Louisiana. During his tenure as mayor, he was an active leader of the school system and presided over its expansion from one to six schools. Neville High School was constructed during his administration.

Arnold strove for racial equality and improved race relations in his part of Louisiana. This was a time when lynchings and extreme violence against African Americans were at their height, and he was determined to put a stop to it. Mayor Bernstein considered himself to be a minority member, since he was Jewish. He refused the Ku Klux Klan a permit to march in parades in downtown Monroe during the 1920s. Mayor Bernstein paid for the college education of one of Ouachita parish's esteemed educators, Henry Carroll (namesake of Carroll High School). Henry Carroll was of Black heritage, became a leading educator in Munroe, spokesman for blacks, a teacher, a football coach, and eventually the principal during the 1940s. He made such an impression on the community that the high school was named after him in 1953. Mayor Bernstein also endorsed the business of African Americans in Monroe, most notably the medical practice of Dr. J.T. Miller and Dr. J.C. Roy.

Arnold died suddenly on December 21, 1937, at his home on 819 North Second Street while still serving as the Mayor of Monroe. There were no premonitions of the mayor's approaching end. He had spent the evening at a dinner party with Mrs. Bernstein, and later several social hours at the home of Mr. and Mrs. Edgar Florsheim. At eleven o'clock, the mayor and Mrs. Bernstein arrived at the North Second street home. Preparations for retirement were leisurely, with no warning of untoward events, until shortly after midnight the mayor was seized with a sudden choking in his throat. The mayor's personal physician hurried to the residence after being called, but medical aid was ineffective. Arnold apparently realized his end was near and his last words to his wife were, "I'm going." At 12:40, he passed into coma, and ten minutes later, Mayor Bernstein breathed his last. Physicians gave the cause of death as acute congestive heart failure.

He was interred in the Monroe Jewish Cemetery. His wife, Corinne (Steinau) Bernstein, died February 9, 1955, and is interred beside her husband.

Arnold's obituary in The Monroe Morning World, December 22, 1937

"A Prince has Fallen in Israel ... Floral Tributes Expressive of Esteem in Which Mayor was Held"

The entire city of Monroe, as well as citizens from all parts of the state paid tribute to Mayor Arnold Bernstein Wednesday afternoon during impressive funeral services held in Temple B'Nai Israel and at the Jewish Cemetery.

Hundreds unable to gain admittance to the flower-banked temple, stood in the pouring rain outside the edifice as the services were conducted by Rabbi F.K. Hirsch.

The temple rostrum was literally transformed into a mountain of floral tributes expressing the esteem with which Mayor Bernstein was held throughout the state. Conspicuous was the head of the casket, covered with a blanket of beautiful blooms was a magnificent wreath mounted on a tall pedestal with a floral base sent by Governor and Mrs. R.W. Loche.

Not in all the years of his service in the exalted position he held has any word or act of his brought discredit to his name or to the name of the community. In the heat of political controversy unkind things may have been said, but today in the presence of all that is mortal of a great leader, this is nothing but testimony of the universal regard and esteem in which he was held by everyone with whom he came in contact. As a public servant he was a shining light. He loved the city and its people, not the office he held, which he accepted as the means by which he could render devoted and unselfish service.

Those who were close and dear to him in the ties of family relationships are not alone in the grief that befalls with his passing. Ours is a community grief, and it is ours to comfort each other in a common sorrow. To her who shared so much with him and gave him courage to meet his heroic task, you walk not alone. Each of us shares your sorrow and will serve you and love you as we did him.

Arnold Bernstein was not a religionist in the ordinary sense of the term. He was so religious he had not time for religion. He lived to make others happy and his heart and his hand were invariably available to those who needed his counsel and his help. His was a genuine, practical and consistent religion.

His life was one to inspire emulation – to invoke the prayer, "Let me die the death of the righteous: let my end be like theirs."

Rabbi Hirsch in his address paid eloquent tribute to the life and service of Mayor Bernstein. The address was based on the words from I Samuel 3:38 'Behold, today a prince is fallen in Israel.' Arnold Bernstein was a prince not only in Israel, but in the community which he served. He was a nobleman of the highest rand, trustworthy, honest sincere and devoted to the interests of the people. You should be thinking of a monument to his memory and that thought will do you credit, but no monument of marble or granite or bronze, no shaft that would rear itself to the skies would adequately represent his accomplishments. The real monument to his memory would be the bringing to fulfillment of his unfinished tasks and making this community all that Arnold Bernstein desired it to be. Such a monument, imperishable in the hearts of men would endure through the ages for the betterment of the future generations of the people he loved.

Uniformed members of the police and fire departments served as ushers and as the throng assembled in the temple the organ played by Leon Hammonds rendered soft music. Mayor Bernstein was buried in the Monroe Jewish Cemetery. Along the route to the ceremony thousands stood with bared heads as the long funeral procession wended its way to the burial place.

Corinne's obituary in The Monroe Morning World, February 13, 1955

"A Gracious Woman is No More"

The passing of Corinne Steinau Bernstein, widow of one of Monroe's most beloved mayors, has left a place that can never be filled in Monroe. This fine woman spent the entire 75 years of her life in Monroe and played an important role in the life of the city. She was an especially gracious woman which well fitted her for the role of first lady of Monroe during the longest period that any mayor in the city's history has filled the post as its chief executive.

She was deeply interested in the city, in Temple B'nai Israel and in her numerous friends. She was willing to sacrifice for them and her charities were numerous, but never did she desire to disclose what she did for other who needed her aid.

"She loved deeply, and was deeply loved," declared Rabbi F.K. Hirsch from Temple B'nai Israel at her ceremony. "There was no end to her love and no one was beyond its influence. With no children of her own, she took to her heart the children of her brothers and sisters. She was mother to her nieces and nephews, and still more she mothered her brothers and sisters. She was always greatly concerned about them, and I am sure that could she have had her way, she would have been the last to go so that she could comfort them to the end.

I can well recall, how this grand first lady of Monroe, during the war, threw open her house to boys at Selman Field and even had one of them married in her home. She delighted in doing for them as she did for other and her neighbors shared in the wealth of love which was hers. I think of her as 'The First Lady of Goodwill.'

She was not a church goer as are many folks, but she lived a religion of love, understanding, service, kindness and cheer. Hers was a practical religion. Her memory will long remain with us. We will recall her graciousness with joy, her charm, her affection and her happiness. It is hoped that some of us may follow her example and throw open our hearts and our homes to those who come our way and for those we love."

Arnold Bernstein 1874-1937

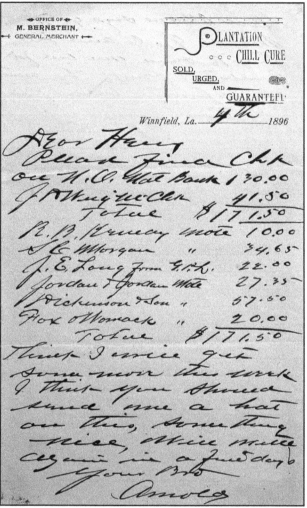

Letter from Arnold to Henry Bernstein Sr. at 24 yrs. & working at Uncle Morris store.

Arnold Bernstein on left at Democratic Convention

Bernstein Park, Monroe, Louisiana—Arnolds vision fulfilled

Arnold Bernstein on left at the early Bernstein Park
(Called Bernstein Folly by his opposition)

Arnold Bernstein 1874-1937

Mrs. Arnold Bernstein

News-Star-World Thursday, March 31, 1983

ACCENT

Arnold & Corrine Bernstein are both buried in the Jewish Cemetery in Monroe, Louisiana

Bernstein's foresight shaped Monroe

Editor's note: First in a series of twice weekly articles detailing contributions of the Jewish community to northeastern Louisiana.

By BETTY McMILLAN
Staff Writer

Arnold Bernstein, 15th mayor of Monroe, was a man with foresight.

But he wasn't a man everyone agreed with. He saw a large city with a demand for recreational areas. His contemporaries saw the action he took to meet that need as "Bernstein's Folly."

The "folly" was 147 acres of land, located between Standifer and Thomas streets, east of Wilson Street, which he purchased for the city on Sept. 17, 1928, at a cost of $42,642. His friends called the purchase a folly because it was in a low area of the city and populated with nothing but a bunch of pin oak trees.

The land, bought from the Biedenharn and Terzio families, has, in less than 60 years, turned into the tourist attraction known today as Louisiana Purchase Gardens and Zoo. Bernstein had recognized the city's potential and the needs it would have in years to come.

Bernstein was the son of a family that was among Louisiana's earliest settlers. The family first settled near Alexandria, then moved on to Grant and Winn parishes. It was in 1874 in Montgomery, Grant Parish, that Arnold Bernstein was born. His father had served as an officer in the Confederate Army, according to "Who's Who in the Twin Cities," written by H.H. Brinsmade. The mayor's mother lived to an advanced age and was still living in Grant Parish in 1931 when the book was published.

Arnold Bernstein was educated in public schools and was a graduate of Soule College in New Orleans. He moved to Monroe in 1905 and married the former Corinne Steinan. Their family home was located at 819 N. Second St. Monroe.

Arnold Bernstein

"He was successfully engaged in the insurance business, first with New York Life Insurance Company and later with Equitable Life Insurance Company.

"He first served as an alderman for Monroe and was elected mayor in 1919, holding the position continually until he died in office in 1937. His election in 1927 was in an unopposed campaign, a feat that had not been accomplished before in Monroe," Brinsmade said in his book.

During his terms in office Monroe experienced its greatest industrial and commercial growth to that time, due, in part, to Bernstein's foresight.

He was a member of the Chamber of Commerce, Rotary Club and Lotus Club, and an active member of the local Jewish synagogue then located in downtown Monroe.

He was chairman of the executive committee of the Tensas Basin Flood Control Association and assisted with federal flood control programs in northeastern Louisiana.

Mayor Bernstein was an active leader of the school system and presided over its expansion from one to six schools. Neville High School was constructed during the Bernstein administration.

Not only did his "park folly" turn into a Monroe attraction, but during the Great Depression a public garden was maintained, according to "Monroe History" by Grigsby, (whose first name isn't given in the book) written in 1936. "Here vegetables are cultivated and given to people in necessitatious circumstances who will go after them. Potatoes, beans, cabbage, greens and all the common variety of vegetables are raised and sometimes as many as 40 families are supplied with vegetables in a single day."

The mayor had established a nursery where trees and flowering shrubs were cultivated. The winding mile-long lagoon in Bernstein Park was a project of the Work Projects Administration in the 1930s.

Directions in the Grigsby book to the park read "Take the Missouri Pacific bus (fare 5 cents) to the park or drive out Jackson Street as far as Standifer, then turn east."

The zoo was moved from Forsythe Park to Bernstein Park in 1936 becasue of flood waters and the building of the levee. By this time the zoo had some 75 species of animals including monkeys, wolves, bobcats, elk, buffalo, deer, bears and alligators.

Bertha Bernstein: 1876–1936

Bertha was born on October 3, 1876, in Montgomery, Louisiana. In 1896, Bertha moved to Monroe after attending teachers' college and immediately became a teacher with the public schools for the next seventeen years.

Bertha married Marcus Kaliski on October 28, 1903. Marcus was an acclaimed jeweler of Monroe. He was in the jewelry business in Monroe for almost half a century at the time of his death. His jewelry company was located at 125 South Grand Street in Monroe. Born in Louisiana, he was the son of one of the early settlers to the region. Initially apprenticing in one of the older established Monroe jewelry stores, Marcus went on to open a very successful jewelry store of his own. Sandra Blate of the Temple B'nai Israel members still has a little turtle pin from his store, shown on the following photo page.

Bertha taught at St. Christopher's day school and was an active member of Temple B.nai Israel. At 8:00 a.m., June 21, 1936, on her way from Monroe to a progressive education course at the Polytechnic Institute in Ruston, Bertha was in a fatal car accident and died on the scene. In the opinion of the corner, the accident was caused by the driver endeavoring to bring the car back on the pavement after one of the front wheels dropped to the shoulder of the road. It occurred on a slight curve in the highway, where eleven other serious accidents had occurred, wearing down the shoulder of the road. The car went out of control, hit the guard rail, bounced back to the railing on the right side, and overturned. Bertha was a much-loved teacher, and after the accident, the Faulk Library in Monroe was dedicated to her to show how much the community loved her. Her brother, Arnold Bernstein, was Mayor of Monroe at the time. The couple are buried together at the Monroe Jewish Cemetery.

The couple had one daughter, Rosalia (Bobby) Kaliski, born February 2, 1906, who married Ferdinand (Bill) Goldsmith on November 30, 1930. Bill Goldsmith was also a jeweler and ran Bobby's father's jewelry store after his death. Bill Goldsmith was the grandson of the Mr. Goldsmith that met Rosalia Budislofski's ship in New Orleans. When Bobby's grandmother, Rosalia, landed in New Orleans, Louisiana by ship in the mid-1850s, it was Mr. Goldsmith who met her and took her to Samuel Bernstein's home, where she met and married Phillip Bernstein.

Rosalia was named after her grandmother but always went by the name Bobby. She attended Newcombe College at Tulane University in New Orleans, where her Uncle Albert Manassas Bernstein graduated medical school, and her Uncle Henry graduated from law school. Bobby went on to be a grade six schoolteacher at St. Christopher's Day School in Monroe and a member of the Louisiana Retired

Teachers Association. Sandra Blate, the historian from Temple B'nai Israel and long-time resident of Monroe, has fond memories of Bobby as her schoolteacher.

CB CB CB

Bertha Bernstein 1876 - 1936 & Family

Kalaski-Bernstein.

Mr. Marcus Kalaski of this city and Miss Bertha Bernstein of Winnfield were united in marriage in the parlor of the Hotel Caddo in Shreveport yesterday afternoon at 2:30 o'clock, Rabi Jacobs officiating. Only relatives and a few intimate friends were present. Mrs. Frank Caspari of this city, sister of the groom, attended.

Mr. Kalaski is a son of Hon. J. L. Kalaski of this city and a prominent and successful young business man, being one of our leading jewelers. He is a member of the parish school board.

The bride is the daughter of Mr. Philip Bernstein of Winnfield and a sister of Mr. Henry Bernstein, a leading member of the Monroe bar. She is an accomplished young lady and for two or three years was one of the most popular teachers in the Monroe High School.—Monroe Daily Star of Thursday.

MARCUS KALISKI RITES ARE HELD

Funeral Conducted On Tuesday Afternoon For Prominent Jeweler

Marcus Kaliski, 68, well-known Monroe jeweler, died yesterday afternoon at 1:30 o'clock at a local sanitarium after an illness of several weeks.

Mr. Kaliski, who was a brother-in-law of the late Mayor Arnold Bernstein of Monroe, had been engaged in the jewelry business here for almost half a century. His establishment M Kaliski Jewelry company, is located at 125 South Grand street.

He was born September 2, 1872, a son of the late J. L. Kaliski one of Monroe's early settlers. He was educated in the public schools here and then began his life's work as an apprentice in the old Monroe jewelry firm that was headed by W. D. Chister.

At the end of his apprenticeship, Mr. Kaliski went into business for himself, opening the jewelry establishment that has been located at the same address for approximately 40 years.

His wife, a former Barkdull Faulk grammar school teacher, was killed four years ago in an automobile accident near Calhoun. The Barkdull Faulk library has since been dedicated to Mrs. Kaliski.

Mr. Kaliski is survived by one daughter, Mrs. Rosalia Goldsmith, a teacher at Barkdull Faulk school, and two brothers, Henry and Julius Kaliski.

Funeral services were held this aft-

The Monroe News-Star.
June 22, 1936
Page 1; Column 1
Monroe Teacher Killed, 3 Hurt
Death Victim is Sister of Local Mayor

Mrs. Marcus Kaliski an instructor in the city for many years. One member of the Barkdull Faulk school faculty was fatally injured and three more hurt, one seriously, when the automobile in which they were traveling overturned early Monday morning on the Dixie Overland highway, three miles east of Ruston. Said to have suffered a fractured skull, Mrs. Marcus Kaliski of 217 Ouachita Avenue, sister of Mayor Arnold Bernstein of Monroe, died before she could be rushed to a Ruston hospital.

The accident occurred about 8 a.m. while the four teachers were on their way from Monroe to Louisiana Polytechnic Institute at Ruston to observe a progressive education course at that institution. Mrs. Duncan was driving the automobile, according to Coroner H. N. Harper of Lincoln parish. In his opinion, the accident was caused by the driver's endeavoring to bring the car back on the pavement after one of the front wheels had dropped to the shoulder of the road. The machine was said to have gone out of control, to have hit the guard railing on the left side of the highway, to have bounced back to the railing on the right side and to have then overturned.

Bertha & Marcus Kaliski - their daughter Bobby Goldsmith & husband Bill are buried in the Munroe Jewish

Turtle brooch from the Kaliski Jewelery Store - Image courtesy of Sandra Blate, Temple B'nai Israel

Bill-Rosalia-Jay Goldsmith 1906-1975 Berth's daughter

Rosalia (Bobby) Goldsmith attended Newcomb College, New Orleans

Albert Manassas Bernstein: 1862–1897

Albert Manassas was my great-grandfather.

When Albert Manassas was born on March 11, 1862, the family commemorated the Confederate victory at the First Battle of Manassas with Albert's second name. The battle took place July 21, 1861. From 1866 to the early 70s, Albert and Henry lived with their Uncle Samuel and Aunt Charlotte in New Orleans, where they attended Jackson Boys' Academy. During the summer months, Albert returned to his parents in Montgomery, Louisiana accompanied by a little French piano that had been brought off a sunken steamship. The piano would travel back and forth with him between school and home each time. While going to school in New Orleans, he took private music lessons from a German professor of music. His brother, Henry, also took fiddle lessons from the same professor. Both brothers graduated from Tulane University; Albert with a degree in medicine and Henry with a degree in law.

In the 1880 census, at eighteen years old and the oldest in the family, Albert is living and working with his Uncle Morris in Winnfield, Louisiana as a clerk in the store. They were both boarders on the farm home of David Dunn in Winnfield, Louisiana. This is before Albert goes to New Orleans Medical College, where he graduated.

On Wednesday, October 18, 1882, Albert married my great-grandmother, Florence Moseley, two days after he was to started classes at medical school. It's not known where they married, but it's speculated that they may have eloped in New Orleans, where Albert was going to medical school. The marriage was not received well by Florence's father, but Albert's parents welcomed Florence into the family. There was still a degree of prejudice against inter-religious marriages at that time.

In 1883, Albert graduated with a medical degree from the University of Louisiana, which became Tulane University. The couple then moved back home and opened his medical practice in Montgomery, Louisiana. It is said that the couple had a plantation on the Cane River in Red River Parish, Louisiana, where all their children were born.

Doctors of the time often owned a combination drug store and dry goods store to supplement their income. On September 26, 1884, Albert had an advertisement in the local newspaper, *The Southern Sentinel*, to promote his store.

Albert Manassas Bernstein add for store

On July 9, 1897, during one of the many epidemics to hit Louisiana, Albert died at the age of only thirty-five. (Lou Harrison's grandmother, Sadie, said he died of cholera, but yellow fever was also rampant in the South.) He is buried in the Jewish Cemetery at Pineville, Louisiana. Florence and Albert had six children. Florence and the children continued to live in Winnfield area for seven years before immigrating to Canada.

Albert Manassas Bernstein & Florence Moseley ~Family Chart

Albert B. Wilkerson *(died during surgery)*
b. Nov 28, 1903, Alabama - d. Sept 8, 1938
Jessie Wilkerson Jr. *(in WWII army for 6 yr)*
b. Jan 8, 1906 , Alabama - b. Dec 12, 1982
Nettie Wilkerson (Elementary School Teacher)
b. May 8,1911, Alabama d. Jun 20, 1987

Albert William (Bernes) Bernstein
b. Sept 21,1912 Clyde, Ohio - d. Aug 14, 1999
Louise Aileen (Bernes) Bernstein
b. Jan 28, 1914, Cleveland - d. Nov 14, 2000

Julian Albert Larocque (m.Beatrice Thomas)
b. Jul 19, 1910, Hamilton, ON - May 15, 1983
Leah Florence Larocque (m.John Duffy)
b. June 28,1912 Hamilton, ON - Apr 26, 2000
Florence May Larocque (m.George Gignac)
b. Sept 22, 1913, Hamilton, ON - Oct 17, 1996
Gerard Soloman Larocque (m. C Gauthier)
b. Feb 14, 1922 Espanola - Mar 4, 1959
Charlotte B. Larocque (m.Joseph Tilly)
b. Oct 21,1923, Espanola - Oct 5, 2000

Albert Reginald Chiswell (m.Marg Daley)
b. Mar.11,1911, Espanola,ON - Apr.19,1969
Ralph Morris Chiswell (Peggy Price)
b. Mar 3,1915 Coniston, ON - Feb.11,1982
Edith Albertina Chiswell (m. Cecil Johnson)
b. Nov 2 1919, Coniston,ON - Oct 13, 1985
Audrey Ann Chiswell (m. Jack Trotter)
b. June 27,1931, Coniston,ON - Mar 31 2003

Albert Morris Bernstein(Burns)(m.R. Morrison)
b. Sept 8, 1931, Port Robinson,ON - d.Mar 24,2013
- children: Bryan & Kathryn
Irene Bernstein (m.Gerrard Kerr)(Leonard Davidson)
b.May 28, 1933
- children: Kim & Karen

Mary Louise Corner (m. Avila Michaud)
-3 children
b. Aug 5, 1916, Hamilton ON - Oct 26, 1975
Morris Lloyd Corner
b. Jun 11, 1918 Thorold, ON - Dec 16, 1937
Aubrey Joseph Corner (m. Phyllis Church Stringer)
b. Jul 22, 1921 Thorold, ON - 1965

Married ~ Jessie E.Wilkerson
b. Apr 16, 1873 Alabama, USA
d. Dec 30, 1933 Hartford, Geneva, Alabama USA
m.#1 Feb 2, 1903 Geneva, Alabama USA
m.#2 **Mr. Holman?**

Augusta (Gussie) Bernstein
b. Nov 3,1885, Red River Parish, Louisiana US
d. Aug 21, 1972, Tombstone, Arizona US

Married ~ Charlotte Elizabeth Howes
b. Apr 11, 1875 Carleton, ON
d. Jan 21, 1945, Hamilton, ON
m. Dec. 31, 1906, Ottawa, ON
m. **Mary Margaret Percha** (Trudnowski)
b. Mar 31, 1891 Erie, NY US
d. Sept 1973 New Hyde Park, NY US
m. Jun 4, 1917 - Tonawanda, NY

Henry Otto Bernstein
b. Mar 1,1888 Red River Parish, Louisiana US
- auto salesman- died in World War I army
d. September 12, 1918, Lorraine, France

St. Mihiel
American
Cemetery
France

Married ~ George Henri J. Larocque
b. Dec 20, 1885, St. Andre, PQ
d. Aug 14, 1947, Iroquois Falls, ON
m. Aug 23, 1909, Espanola, ON
Occupation: *worked in Abitibie paper mill*

Sadie Edith Bernstein
b. Apr 23,1890, Red River Parish, Louisiana US
d. September 29, 1983, Iroquois Falls, ON

Married ~ Aubrey Reginald Chiswell
b. Jul 3, 1887 Brantford/Paris, ON
d. Sept. 1940, Sudbury, ON
m. Feb 6, 1910,Webbwood, ON
Occupation:CNR Station Master, Coniston, ON

Charlotte Amelda Bernstein
b. Oct 13,1892 Cane River County, Louisiana US
d. Jan 7, 1960 Coniston, ON Canada

Married ~ Elisabeth Teutenberg
b. Feb 26, 1904 Bruhl, Germany
d. Mar 31, 2011, Port Robinson, ON
m. July 25, 1923 Toronto, York ON

Joseph Maurice Albert Bernstein
b. Nov 10,1894, Red River Parish, Louisiana US
d. February 27, 1978, Welland, ON
Occupation: *Electrician at Standard Steel*

Married ~ Joseph Corner
b. May, 1895 Richmond, PQ
d. Dec 31, 1965 Florida, US *(on vacation)*
m. Oct 12, 1915 Espanola, ON

Minna Bernstein
b. Feb 10, 1897, Red River Parish, Louisiana US
d. Jul 20, 1961 Thorold South, ON

Albert's Father: Phillip Bernstein
b. Apr 10, 1827 Gnesen,Posen,Prussian Poland
immigrated 1843 (1910 US census)
d. Jul 7, 1911 Winnfield, Louisiana, AL USA
m. Jul 12, 1859 Montgomery, Louisiana, AL USA
Albert's Mother: Rosalia (Budislofski) Marks
b. May 10, 1840 Posen,Thueringen, Prussia
d. May 5, 1931 Winnfield, Louisiana, AL USA

Rosalina
Bernstein

Phillip
Bernstein

Dr. Albert Manassas Bernstein
b. March 11, 1862, Winnfield, Louisiana US
d. July 9, 1897, Winnfield, Louisiana US
- died at age 35 during a cholera epidemic
Occupation: doctor
Married ~ Florence Moseley
b. September 22, 1866, Sylacauga, Alabama
immigrated to Canada 1904 after 7 year as a widow
d. Jul 31, 1950, St. Catharines, ON
m. Oct 18, 1882 *(not known where)*
m. **Jean Baptiste Labelle**
b. Jun 16, 1860 St. Jerome, PQ
(3 children from previous marriage to Mary McFerson)
d. Oct 11, 1933, Sault Ste Marie, ON
m. Aug 14, 1904, Pembroke, ON

Florence
Moseley

William
Moseley

Florence's Father: William Jordan Moseley
b. Apr 19, 1840 Dallas, Alabama USA
Mar 10, 1862 recruited; confederate Cahawba rifles AL
d. June 6, 1896, Andalusia, Alabama USA
Florence's Mother: Sophronia Goodwin
b. abt. 1847, Alabama USA
d. abt 1879
m. Dec 16, 1861 Dallas, Alabama USA
- *Sophronia's father Isaiah J. Goodwin 1825- was in the*
1st heavy artillery of the 21 regiment in 1863 during the
Civil War. Mother: Jane 1830-1856
m. #2 **Cynthia Tillis** - Feb 2, 1886 Andalusia, AL
b. Jan 3,1864, Elba, Coffee, Alabama US
d. Jan 14, 1944 Gaskin, Florida US

compiled by trudy chiswell- trudychiswell@fastmail.fm 2021-06-01

Source of information Miles Krisman, Gerry Michaud Ancestry.ca

Dr. Albert Manassas Bernstein 1862-1897

Battle of Manassas (Bull Run)*- 1st battle of the Civil War &Confederate victory*

Street in Old New Orleans, Louisiana where Albert & brother Henry went to school

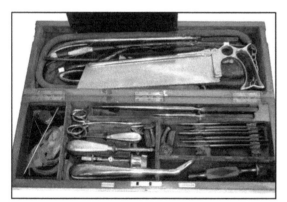

Surgeon's Equipment of those times

Albert Manassas Bernstein - buried Pineville Jewish cemetery, Rapids Parish, Louisiana , row #15

Dr. Albert Manassas Bernstein Family

Life in

Louisiana

USA

Florence collecting eggs on the farm in Louisiana

The Bernstein children before going to Canada in 1904
Back: Henry – Gussie – Sadie & Front: Charlotte – Minna – Morris

Many

years

later in

Canada

back row - Minna & Joe Corner – Morris & Elizabeth Bernstein – George & Sadie Larocque
front row: Charlotte Chiswell – Florence Bernstein/Labelle – Gussie Wilkerson

Florence Moseley: 1866–1950

Story by Gerry Michaud, great-grandson to Florence and grandson to Minna Bernstein Corner. Florence lived with Gerry's family in her old age. Florence was great-grandmother to both Gerry and trudy.

Florence Moseley was born on September 22, 1867, in Sylacauga, Alabama, USA. She was the only child of William Jordan Moseley and Sophronia Godwin. Her mother suffered a number of miscarriages, reputed to be between ten and twelve, and died when Florence was still a small child. Florence's father doted on her, denying her nothing, and as a result, she was quite spoiled. Since her father was a schoolteacher, she was well educated for a young woman of her day and was an accomplished pianist.

When she was only seventeen years of age, Florence ran away from home to marry Albert Bernstein, who was still in medical school at the time. William Moseley disowned his only daughter, who had the audacity to marry a "Jew." The Bernsteins, while displeased that Albert had married while still in school, were far more supportive. Florence lived with Albert's parents while he completed medical school. This spoiled child, who had never worked a day in her life, got a shock of reality when her mother-in-law, Rosalia, handed her a bolt of material and informed her that the women in the Bernstein family made the menfolk's shirts, and she was to do the same. Florence had no experience in practical matters, and it's to be questioned as to the quality of the first few shirts she made for her new husband. She persevered and became an accomplished seamstress, making all of her own clothes and the large aprons that she always wore around the house, even as an elderly woman.

Florence and Albert lived on what is reputed to be a fairly large farm after his graduation. In the summer months, Albert would train young medical students who boarded at the farm. There were a number of workers on the farm, and it happened that when one of them, who is only known to us as Sam, died, Albert placed his remains in a large cauldron in the yard and boiled the flesh from his bones. He then wired them together and used the skeleton as an aid in teaching anatomy. Some of the students liked to play practical jokes, and on more than one occasion, Florence would open a linen closet door to have "Sam" fall out and drape himself around her shoulders!

In addition to practicing medicine, Albert raised racehorses on the farm and grew at least some of his own hay and oats. One story told by Florence was that during the period after Albert's death, some of the Black men in the area would sneak in at night and race the horses, taking bets on the outcome. One dark night during one of these illicit races, Florence covered her head with one of the large white aprons she used to wear, and making a loud noise, surprised and frightened the participants, who never came back to race again. They spread the news that the ghost of Dr. Albert was guarding the farm.

When Albert died in 1897 of the same epidemic virus he was treating his patients for, he left a thirty-two-year-old widow and six children ranging in age from twelve years (Augusta) to baby Minna, who was only five months old.

It's not known exactly when Florence left for Canada in 1904, but she married Jean Baptiste Labelle on August 14, 1904, in Pembroke, Ontario. Gussie got married in 1903 and stayed in Louisiana, as did Henry. The youngest four children went to Canada with their mother in 1904. It was a tragic marriage, as she thought he was a well-to-do lumber baron, only to find out that Jean Baptiste Labelle was a lumberjack, and her new home was a virtual tar paper shack. J.B. had been married before to Mary Isabella McPherson, who died in 1902, and he had three children. Florence and J.B. lived in Pembroke for a short time and then moved to Espanola, Ontario, where the children were to grow up. J.B. Labelle was a shoemaker by trade, and Florence gave him the money to set up a shop in town. Every day Labelle went to work and came home. On a surprise trip to town, Florence passed by the shop only to find it empty and unoccupied. What Labelle spent the money on is not known, but perhaps it went to his other children. The family had to rely on Florence's ability to take in laundry and give piano lessons for income. Florence must have had some money from the sale of the Louisiana farm, but it went quickly to provide for her children, thanks to Labelle's lack of industry. Too ashamed to go back home to Louisiana after her deception, she stayed in Canada and worked hard to provide for her family. According to a letter we found, Florence's brother-in-law, Rudolph (Bootsie) Bernstein, had to send her money to pay the rent a year after she was married on August 15, 1905. It's rather a sad story, but Florence was a strong woman and committed to her children.

Florence and Jean were married in a Catholic church, and she converted to Catholicism, as did the children. The bishop of the diocese baptized the children. This was unusual, as it's normally the parish priest that baptizes children. All of the children remained Catholic except Charlotte, and Florence herself. Miffed by the attitude of her parish priest during confession, she left and returned to the Baptist faith of her childhood.

Florence and Jean Labelle were separated, but she never got a divorce, and she kept the name Labelle throughout the remainder of her life. In addition to Jean Labelle's other faults, he had a drinking problem and was hated by his stepchildren, Morris and Minna.

As she aged, Florence lived for a time with her daughter, Charlotte, and her husband, Aubrey Chiswell, who was the station master for the CNR Coniston, Ontario station. Florence suffered from glaucoma and told the story of how she was walking along the railroad tracks on her way home when the last of her sight went completely, leaving her permanently blind. She lay down on the tracks and cried her heart out. Shortly after this her son-in-law Aubrey died and she went to live with her youngest daughter, Minna, and her husband, Joseph Corner, who had left Espanola to work at the Ontario Paper Co. in Thorold, Ontario. They were living in company housing at the time, later moving to St. Catharines, Ontario during one of Minna and Joe's several separations. They lived on Thomas St. in St. Catharines. While there, Florence acted as midwife for Minna, delivering her twins, Aubrey and Alice. Alice was born breach and didn't survive. Between the time she went blind and her moving to St. Catharines, she had an eyeball surgically removed from its socket. No one now knows why, but she was always pictured wearing dark glasses to hide the deformity. Her great-grandchildren never saw her without them. She loved to read and had a great deal of difficulty in learning "moonstone," the method used by the blind prior to Braille. She promised the Lord that if she could learn to read it, she would read only the Bible. She did learn it and, true to her word, was never seen to read anything else.

When Minna and her husband moved to Thorold South, Florence went to live with her daughter, Charlotte, for a short period, after which she lived with her granddaughter, Louise Corner Michaud, for a few years. She was very independent and mostly kept to her room, where she had an enameled covered cupboard and a hot plate used to heat soup and water for tea. She slept on her goose down mattress and pillows she'd made from goose feathers on the farm in Louisiana. This was the same mattress she had shared with her husband, Albert. While living with Louise, her grandson, Gerry, who was quite a little entrepreneur, always ran errands for her. Gerry remembers that Greaty-Gran would receive her monthly cheque in the mail, and as soon as it was cashed, he would get his allowance for being her errand boy. He would then run to get a butterfly bun from the bakery to eat. There were no direct deposit or bank machines in those days, so someone would have to cash the cheque for Florence.

Florence disliked using the bathroom on a regular basis, so she kept a chamber pot in her room, which she dumped out once or twice a day. When she was getting a glass of water for her great-grandson, Lloyd, who was about four years old at the time, she took a wrong turn and fell down the stairs. While she wasn't seriously hurt, she was badly shaken and subsequently spent her last years living again with her daughter, Minna, because their home in Thorold South was all on one floor. She died there on November 20, 1952, at the age of eighty-five.

CB CB CB

Florence (Moseley) Bernstein 1866-1950

Florence Bernstein with grandchildren at Coniston CNN railway station
Albert Chiswell on left with Larocque children

Gussie, Florence & Charlotte

Charlotte (Bernstein) Chiswell - Florence (Moseley-Bernstein) Labelle & Minna
(Bernstein) Corner on CNN Station, Coniston - at Edith Chiswell wedding

Union Jack - Canada's flag until 1965

Carole Trotter on steps with Florence Labelle, Sadie Larocque with her daughter & granddaughter on R

Florence (Moseley) Bernstein 1866-1950

Letter from Florence to "Buddy" in Louisiana, USA

Pembroke Ont
Sept 7th 1906

Dear Buddy,
I wrote to you some time ago. and cant think why you do not reply. also to Ma. I have the children in school. We are all up but I am not well. and little Minna is very thin. My poor Baby it grieves me to look at her. I had a letter from Henry some time ago. and he is working in a R.R. Shop. My poor Boy. I want to see him so

bad. he writes seldom. and Gussie is just as bad. I hope you are all well. also the folks in Winnfield. Buddy, if you have it to spare could you lend me $10.00 until you draw the balance of the rent. then keep back your money. Minnie needs some shoes & a coat. very badly. and I never shall ask Mr LaBelle for any thing for my children again. Send it you can spare it. Henry could help me too if he would. I am trying to get so

I can't do some sewing and make a few cents. I am reaking my just due. but it wont be for many years. and then I'll be done with this life. I wrote Gussie to write you let me know if she did or not. My poor child. she will soon have an other addition to her family, and I long to be with her. We are having some cold weather already had frost 2 weeks. very little Summer up here. Well I must close. We all send lots

Gussie—Florence—Charlotte Bernstein

of love to all. Write soon. soon.

Lovingly Sister

Florence

Florence (Moseley) Bernstein 1866-1950

Letter from Florence Bernstein/Labelle to "Buddy" Louisiana, USA in 1905 - one year after marrying JB Labelle

Florence's whole family together (missing Henry, who died 1918) Back Row, L to R: Minna & Joe Corner, Morris & Elisabeth Bernstein. George & Sadie Larocque - Front Row L to R: Charlotte Chiswell, Florence Bernstein/Labelle, Gussie Wilkerson

Florence and Albert Bernstein's Children

1. Gussie, 1885–1972

2. Henry, 1888–1918

3. Sadie, 1890–1983

4. Charlotte – 1892 – 1960

5. Morris, 1894–1978

6. Minna, 1897–1961

ଔ ଔ ଔ

WILKINSON RITES SET FOR TODAY

Coffee Springs Native Dies In Cleveland

HARTFORD—Funeral services for Albert B. Wilkinson, thirty-five, of Birmingham, who died Thursday in a Cleveland, Ohio hospital following an operation, will be held at 4 p.m. today at Hartford Baptist church with the Rev. A. D. Zbinden of Dothan officiating, assisted by the Rev. J. H. Dykes of Hartford. Burial will be in the Hartford cemetery with Holman Funeral Home of Hartford directing.

Mr. Wilkinson was a native of Coffee Springs but came to Hartford at an early age. At the time of his death, he was residing in Birmingham where he was connected with Dun and Bradstreet. He was member of the Hartford Baptist church.

Surviving are his wife, mother, Mrs. Gussie B. Wilkinson of Hartford; one sister, Miss Nettie Ruth Wilkinson of Hartford; one brother, Jesse C. Wilkinson, Jr., of Hawaiian Islands.

Active pallbearers will be J. T. Holman, Jack Childs, Keller Williams, Emory Corbitt, Olen Johnson, and Roy Jones. Honorary pallbearers are to be F. E. Brooks, H. B. Snyder, Fred Black, H. E. Singletary, Dick Lacey, Quin Borland, Sr., George Hause and Lewis Johnson.

Augusta (Gussie) Bernstein: 1885–1972

Augusta was born on November 3, 1885, at home in Red River Parish, Louisiana, as were all the children of Albert and Florence. Red River Parish is on the western border of Winn Parish, where the family is said to have a plantation.

The year before her mother moved up to Canada, Gussie married Jesse E. Wilkerson on February 2, 1903, in Geneva, Alabama. The couple moved to Main Street in the town of Coffee Springs, Alabama, where Mr. Wilkerson was a bookkeeper in a retail store. By 1920, they had moved to Hartford Geneva, Alabama, where Jesse was a bookkeeper in a bank, and later in 1930, just before he died, he worked as an insurance writer. He died in 1933 at the age of sixty, leaving Gussie with their three children: Albert, Jesse Jr., and Nettie.

1. Albert: (November 28, 1903–September 8, 1938) died during surgery in Cleveland, Ohio

2. Jesse Jr.: (January 8, 1906–December 12, 1982) served in the Army in WWII from July 3, 1940 to April 30, 1946

3. Nettie Ruth: (May 8, 1911–June 20, 1987) was an elementary school teacher, married William Holland on July 6, 1941

Gussie married again, as it shows her in the 1940 census with the name Holman and still living in Hartford, Alabama and listed as a widow in the census. Her daughter, Nettie, is listed as twenty-eight years old, living with her mother, and working as a teacher. I can't find any marriage license for Mr. Holman, but on Gussie's gravestone is listed both Wilkerson and Holman. It's not known when Gussie moved to Arizona with failing health, but she died in Tombstone, Arizona and was taken back to Hartford, Alabama to be buried by her husband, Jesse E. Wilkerson, in Hartford City Cemetery, plot section 4.

Henry Otto Bernstein: 1888–1918

Henry Otto Bernstein was born on March 1, 1888, at home in Red River Parish, Louisiana.

It's said that after his mother moved to Canada to remarry, Henry stayed in Louisiana with his grandparents, Phillip and Rosalia Bernstein. It's not known why he didn't accompany his mother to Canada. The family story goes on to say that not long after his mother left, Henry ran away from his grandparents to make his way to Canada. Riding freight trains all the way to Canada, he was reunited with his family; however, he didn't get along very well with his stepfather and went out on his own again to work on a railroad survey crew. Henry would have been seventeen years old at the time. Florence, Henry's mother, shared his struggles in a letter to her brother-in-law, Rudolph (Bootsie) Bernstein, on August 9, 1905:

> *"I had a few lines from Henry last week and he is a way up in the Provence of Quebec— working on a Rail Road Survey. I had not heard from him in 2 months. I was so messy about him. My poor boy! My heart is one long string of prayers for my boy in fact for all my poor precious children."* Aug. 9, 1905

Henry married Charlotte Elizabeth Howes on December 31, 1906, in Ottawa. I can't find any further info on the marriage or if there were any children at this time. Later Henry moved to Rochester, New York and then Buffalo. On June 4, 1917, Henry married Mary Margaret Percha, a divorcee with two children, Albert William Bernes and Louise Aileen Bernes, in Buffalo, New York. On June 5, 1917, he enlisted in the US Army and reported that he was married with three children, which makes me wonder if he had a child with Charlotte. Mary's children are:

1. Albert William Bernes: (September 21, 1912–August 14, 1999) was in the Navy in WWII

2. Louise Aileen Bernes: (January 28, 1914–November 14, 2000) married Arthur A Rice and lived in New Hyde Park, New York

During WWI, Henry enlisted in Buffalo for service in the Army. On the draft card under "Do you claim exemption from draft?" Henry put that he was married with three children. Was that why he married the day before going to report for the draft? He was born in the US, so I assume he was eligible to be drafted. His chances of an exemption from the WWI draft were pretty slim, since he served in the Alabama National Guard in Louisiana before coming to Canada. While in the army, Henry served as a private and was initially stationed at Columbus Barracks, Ohio. On July 31, 1918, he was sent overseas and listed as being in the 32nd Provisional Ordinance Battalion. While in France, he contracted pneumonia and died on September 12, 1918. I wonder now if it was really the Spanish Flu that Henry died from, as it was spreading uncontrolled in the army at the time. It was the army coming back from the war that spread the Spanish Flu through the US in 1819. He is buried in the St. Mihiel American Cemetery, Thiaucourt, France, plot A, row 7, grave 28.

CB CB CB

Henry Otto Bernstein 1888-1918

MARRIAGES

County of Carleton   Division of Ottawa

Army registration card - served as a private in WWI

Henry Otto Bernstein died overseas in WWI - buried St. Mihiel American
Cemetery, Thiaucourt, France; plot A – row 7 – grave 28

State of New York

No. 4701	FOR THE GROOM		FOR THE BRIDE	
NAME	Henry Otto Bernstein	COLOR White	Mary Margaret Percha	COLOR White
RESIDENCE	Rochester N.Y.	AGE 29	North Tonawanda	AGE 26
OCCUPATION	Auto Salesman	NO. OF MARRIAGE 1st	maid	NO. OF MARRIAGE 2nd
BIRTHPLACE	Winfield La.	WIDOWER	Buffalo N.Y.	WIDOW no
FATHER	Albert Bernstein	DIVORCED	Joseph Percha	DIVORCED yes
BIRTHPLACE	U.S.	" WHEN	Germany	" WHEN
MOTHER	Florence Mosley	" WHERE	Louise Tittaver	" WHERE Mich.
BIRTHPLACE	U.S.		U.S.	
CONSENT BY		RELATION		RELATION
DATE OF LICENSE June 4, 1917	DATE OF MARRIAGE June 4, 1917	PLACE OF MARRIAGE N. Tonawanda		OFFICIAL H. E. Bayley
PROFESSION Clergyman	WITNESS O. A. Wattengel, I. V. Bayley			

Sadie Edith Bernstein: 1890–1983

Sadie Edith Bernstein was born at home on May 23, 1890, in Red River Parish, Louisiana.

Sadie was fourteen years old when she moved to Canada with her mother in 1904. She worked in a cigar factory in Pembroke, Ontario before her marriage to George Henri Larocque on August 23, 1909, in Espanola, Ontario. It's believed that Sadie also converted to Roman Catholicism at that time, as her husband was also of that faith. The couple had five living children and lost one child. The family eventually moved to Iroquois Falls, Ontario, where they spent the remainder of their lives.

Lou Harrison, Charlotte Larocque's daughter and Sadie's granddaughter, has many fond memories of her Grandfather George, who she said was lovingly called "Grump." George worked in Iroquois Falls Abitibi Paper mill, founded in 1914, all his life. The mill closed in 2016, ending an era of over one hundred years of operation in the town. Lou remembers visiting her grandpa in Northern Ontario when she was a small child. Sadie would make a meal for George to take to work and place it on a ceramic dish, covered with foil. George would take his lunch plate to work and place it near one of the boilers in the mill to keep it warm. The plate and story were passed down to Lou from her mother. A family treasure of fond memories.

After George's death in 1948, Sadie took up Red Cross nursing. She worked in the Hotel Dieu Hospital in St. Catharines, Ontario, finishing off her career as a private nurse. Unfortunately, Sadie developed glaucoma that caused her to go blind by 1977, as her mother did with the same condition. To make matters worse, Sadie also suffered from deafness. She lived with her daughter, Florence, in Iroquois Falls for many years in later life. On September 29, 1983, Sadie died at the age of ninety-four.

The couple was blessed with five children.

1. Julian Albert, July 19, 1910–May 15, 1983: During WWII, he served in the Canadian Army as a member of the Tank Corps. He married Beatrice Thomas, and they had one daughter named Linda.

2. Leah Florence, June 28, 1912–April 26, 2000: Leah married John Edward Duffy on July 6, 1936, in St. Ann's Roman Catholic Church, Iroquois Falls, Ontario. The couple had four children: Beulah Ann, Gerald Edward, Lloyd Albert, and Carol Ann. John Duffy died on May 10, 1975. Leah remained in Iroquois Falls until her death on April 26, 2000.

3. Florence May, September 22, 1913–October 17, 1996: Florence married George Gignac on February 6, 1935, in Iroquois Falls, Ontario at the age of twenty-one. The couple soon moved to Hamilton, Ontario, where they raised their family. Florence's mother, Sadie, lived with her in later years until her death. On October 17, 1996, Florence died in a Windsor, Ontario nursing home. The couple had two children: Beverly and Gloria. Not much else is known of the family at this point.

4. Gerard Soloman, February 14, 1922–March 4, 1959: During WWII, he served in the Canadian Navy on a Corvette. Gerard married Carmelle Gauthier on January 7, 1946. The couple had six children: George, Sharon, Brenda, Michael, Shawn, and Caroline.

5. Charlotte, October 21, 1923–October 5, 2000: She married Joseph Gerard Noel de Tilly on August 24, 1946. The couple have three children: Georgianna, Sue-Ann, and Louise. Not much more is known of the couple at this time.

Sadie Edith Bernstein 1890-1983

Sadie & George Larocque

Abitibi Paper Mill, Iraquois Falls, ON where George Larocque worked and the plate that Sadie put his dinner on to take to work with foil covering

Biography

Mother was born in Montgomery Louisianna in year April 23/1890. Came to Canada when she was 14 yrs old. Worked in cigar factory in Pembroke. Married to George Larocque, lived in Espanola in Iroquois Falls. Had six children and raised five of them. Lost Dad in 1948 and took up Red Cross nursing. Went to Ste. Catherines, nursed in Hotel Dieu Hospital and then did Private nursing. Lost her eyesight from glaucoma and lived many of her years in Iroquois Falls. Last eight years complete blindness, deafness. Lost her youngest son Gerard & oldest son Julian and gave herself into the arms of her Saviour on Sept 29th 1983.

Sadie & George Larocque

Sadie & George Larocque Family

The Larocque Family

Julian & Florence Larocque

Julian & Leah Larocque

Eddy & Leah (Larocque) Duffy

Gerard Larocque

Gerard & Carmelle Larocque

Joseph Gerard Noel de Tilly & Charlotte Larocque

Charlotte Larocque

Charlotte Imelda Bernstein: 1892–1960

Charlotte Imelda Bernstein is the next direct ancestor in my line. Information on her will be in the next section.

Joseph Maurice Bernstein: 1894–1978

Maurice Bernstein was born at home on November 10, 1894, in Red River Parish, Louisiana. In 1904, he moved to Canada with his mother. Initially he lived in Northern Ontario with his mother and stepfather. In the 1921 census, Maurice is living in Espanola with his mother, Florence, and working as an electrician. It says that Florence and Morris obtained their Canadian citizenship in 1909. Maurice was called Morris but always signed his name as the French spelling Maurice.

Maurice later moved to Southern Ontario, where he married Elisabeth Teutenburg on July 25, 1923, in Toronto, Ontario. The couple moved to Port Robinson, and Maurice worked as an electrician at Standard Steel in Port Robinson, Ontario. Their first child, Albert Maurice, was born in Welland on September 8, 1931, and their second child, Irene Ann, was born on May 28, 1933, in Port Robinson.

The family is well remembered by both Gerard Michaud, the grandson of Maurice's sister, Minna, and trudy chiswell, granddaughter of Charlotte, another sister to Maurice. Gerard said of his Great-Uncle Maurice, "He was the nicest and kindest man it has been my pleasure to know." He also recalls that his Great-Aunt Elisabeth was a wonderful cook and baker, always having treats for those who may have stopped by unexpectedly. Elisabeth had a very large Hummel figure collection that was always a fascination to trudy when they visited. The couple's daughter, Irene, and granddaughter, Karen, have the Hummel collection now. Maurice and Elisabeth were a very patient couple, allowing trudy to tinker on their piano when visiting. The couple had two children.

1. Albert Morris Bernstein, September 8, 1931, in Port Robinson, Ontario
2. Irene Ann Bernstein, May 28, 1933, in Port Robinson, Ontario

Maurice died on February 27, 1978, and Elisabeth on March 31, 2011. The couple are both buried together in Holy Cross Cemetery, Welland, Ontario, section 10, row 20.

Joseph Maurice Bernstein 1894-1978

Albert 1931-2013 son

Maurice & Elisabeth Bernstein

Irene 1933 - living - daughter

*1953 Albert—about 21 years old with RCAF
Albert always loved airplanes &
flew for both RCAF & Air Canada*

*Irene Ann Bernstein 1933
Irene loved ballet*

*Elisabeth & Maurice Bernstein's 50th wedding anniversary with
Maurice's sister Sadie Larocque*

AIR CANADA

Bryan & Albert Burns on Elisabeth Bernstein's—100th birthday

Elisabeth Teutenberg Bernstein's 104th birthday

1953 ~ Maurice & Elisabeth Bernstein
Children's Weddings ~ Albert & Irene's

April 11, 1953 - Irene & mother Elisabeth Bernstein

April 11, 1953 - Irene & Gerard Jude Kerr marry

October 3, 1953 - Albert Bernstein & Rosemarie Morrison marry

October 3, 1953 - Albert Bernstein & Rosemarie Morrison wedding reception

Albert Morris Bernstein: 1931–2013

Albert attended Catholic school, graduating from Notre Dame High School in Welland. As a boy, Albert is said to have had a number of model planes about his room. It's not surprising that he went on to become a jet pilot in the Royal Canadian Air Force during the 1950s, flying F-86 "Sabre" jet aircraft. He married RoseMarie Morrison on October 3, 1953, at St. Denis Roman Catholic Church in St. Catharines. The couple had two children.

1. Bryan Albert Burns, September 24, 1954, St. Catharines, Ontario (Hotel Dieu Hospital)
2. Kathryn Elizabeth Burns, July 16, 1956, Baden-Soellingen, West Germany (RCAF Base Hospital)

Albert was stationed in West Germany for three years and then went to Moose Jaw, Saskatchewan, Canada as a flight instructor for two years. After finishing his military flying career, Albert carried on flying as a pilot for Air Canada, living in Montreal, Quebec, where his son, Bryan, still lives today. At about this time, Albert changed his last name from Bernstein to Burns. Although he doesn't recall any overt discrimination against himself due to his Jewish name, discrimination was still prevalent throughout society at the time. A Jewish name such as Bernstein was enough to limit one's prospects in many facets of life. Since he and his family were not Jewish, it was an unnecessary encumbrance to maintain, so the change was made. Albert had a very successful career with Air Canada, flying primarily Boeing 727s. In later years, he served as a "check pilot," ensuring the safety of the fleet. He retired to Burlington, Ontario, and died on March 24, 2013.

Bryan Albert Burns, September 24, 1954

Growing up during the first five years of his life on a military base, Bryan has always had a love of planes, like his dad, Albert. When the family was in Germany, he remembers living across the street from the air base. One day when he was three or four years old, he crossed the street, shimmied under the fence and guard booth, and went for a stroll on the tarmac. Suddenly, guards were shouting the alarm when they saw a little boy out on the tarmac where jets landed. His mother was understandably frantic. The love of planes never died, and Bryan spent a forty-year career as an Air Canada pilot, staying in Montreal, Quebec all his life and into his retirement.

Bryan married Maureen MacDonald, born November 27, 1953. The couple married on February 7, 1976, at home in Dollard des Ormeux, Quebec, and had two children.

1. Scott MacDonald Burns, June 3, 1977, Montreal, Quebec, Canada

2. Roberta Marie Burns, October 4, 1980, Montreal, Quebec, Canada

Kathryn Elizabeth, July 16, 1956

Kathryn married Bradley Allan Doey on January 13, 1979, in St. Raphael Roman Catholic Church in Burlington, Ontario. The couple lived in Ancaster, Ontario initially and then moved up to Collingwood, Ontario in 1988. Kathryn was a math teacher before retirement, and Bradley was a developer/coordinator of a diploma and degree Professional Golf Management Program at Georgian College, Barrie, Ontario. The couple had two children.

1. Bryce Joseph Doey, May 20, 1984, Hamilton, Ontario, Canada

2. Laura Elizabeth Doey, June 21, 1986, Hamilton, Ontario, Canada

Albert & RoseMarie Burns Family, L-R: Brad, Kathy, Bryce, Albert, Laura, RoseMarie, Maureen, Robyn, Bryan, and Scott

Irene Ann Bernstein, 1933–living

Irene attended Catholic school, graduating from Notre Dame High School in Welland. Interested in dance as a child, Irene studied ballet and later went on to teach the neighborhood children who wanted to learn dance. Irene shared memories of her parents driving her to ballet lessons in Welland every Saturday. At eleven years old, she would come home after lessons to a house full of all the neighborhood Port Robinson girls who wanted to learn to dance. Irene would teach them what she had just learned. Once a year they would all gather together and Irene would organize a performance at the Guild Hall in Port Robinson. They would charge 25¢, with the money going to the local baseball diamond. Irene's dad, Maurice, manager of the baseball team, was intent on getting lights around the baseball diamond and bleachers so they could have night games.

Irene married Gerard "Gerry" Jude Kerr, her high school sweetheart, on April 11, 1953, in Immaculate Conception Roman Catholic Church, Port Robinson, Ontario. Gerard loved flying and was a pilot in the Royal Canadian Air Force (RCAF). Soon after the couple married, they boarded a ship, sailing to England, where Gerard was stationed for one and a half years. This was Irene's first time away from the close-knit family town of Port Robinson.

Their son Kim was born in Oakham, England before they were transferred again to France for another year and a half and finally transferred to RCAF Chatham, New Brunswick in Canada. It was from this station that Gerard was selected to be part of the newly formed Golden Hawks Aerobatic flying team. In 1959, the team was formed to celebrate the thirty-five-year anniversary along with fifty years of powered aviation in Canada. The team was chosen based on their flying skills and for their ability to adequately represent the Air Force to the people of Canada. While they were at RCAF Station, Chatham, New Brunswick, their daughter Karen was born.

1. Kim Christopher Kerr, January 22, 1954, Okham, Rutland, England, married Jane Noiles on July 3, 1992

2. Karen Elizabeth Kerr, August 8, 1958, Chatham, New Brunswick, Canada; has a daughter, Jessica Elisabeth, and one granddaughter, Piper Elisabeth

Unfortunately, Gerard was killed in a tragic air accident when flying with the team on August 10, 1959. I remember going to the funeral, and even as a sixteen year old, it was a heart-wrenching funeral, with the twenty-one gun salute at the grave site. After the funeral, Irene went by train back to New Brunswick to close up the house. Crushed at Gerard's early death, Irene said it took her two years to recover. Crying on the train back, Irene was comforted by an older lady sitting next to her. She gave some advice that Irene followed: "Go back to your home town, dear, and buy the cheapest house on the best street in town." After closing the house in New Brunswick and traveling by train back to Ontario, Irene did just that. She purchased a house in Welland. Having just retired, her parents moved in with the little family to help raise the children, who were four and one at the time of their father's death. Karen never knew her father, and Irene's father, Maurice, was like a father to her all her growing up years. He even passed on his love of horses to her.

Fierce, Fiery Warriors Fought Upon the Clouds

From Veterans Affairs web site

> *Flight Lieutenant Kerr lost his life when his North American F-86 'Sabre' V23073 jet aircraft crashed. His "Golden Hawks" Sabre was making a landing at McCall Airfield in Calgary, Alberta with the rest of the "Golden Hawks" aerobatic team, when it collided with a Piper 'Pacer' aircraft while turning, about two miles west of the field. The Pacer had not been authorized to enter the control zone; both occupants in the smaller aircraft also perished in the accident. Gerard was the son of Victor and Winnifred Kerr. He left behind his wife Irene Ann Kerr and two children Kim Christopher and Karen Elizabeth.*
>
> *The Golden Hawks were a Royal Canadian Air Force aerobatic flying team established in 1959 to celebrate the 35th anniversary of the RCAF and the "Golden" 50th anniversary of Canadian flight, which began with Alexander Graham BELL's Aerial Association (AEA) Silver Dart in 1909.*[10]

Irene was alone for nineteen years before she remarried. Meeting her future husband on a visit to her brother Albert's home in Montreal, she eventually married Leonard "Lee" Davidson in April of 1978 at Sacred Heart Church in Delta, British Columbia. Lee also loved airplanes as a navigator in the air force, later working as a mechanical technician on planes for Canadian Pacific Air Lines, which was taken over by Air Canada in 2000. Lee was also an inventor and created a little gizmo that was used to check the aircraft for maintenance. It's still used on all aircraft today. The couple lived in Delta, British Columbia for many years. Irene's mother, Elisabeth, lived with the couple from age 100 until her death at 107 years old. When Lee was eighty, the couple moved back to Fort Erie, Ontario to be near Irene's children. Irene has one grandchild, Jessica, and a great-granddaughter, Piper. Her daughter Karen owns a horse rescue farm a short ten-minute drive from Irene.

Albert Morris Bernstein (Burns) 1931-2013

Albert at RCAF survival training, North Bay, ON
& in RCAF uniform

1953 Albert—about 21 years old with RCAF
Always loved airplanes - flew for both RCAF & Air Canada

Albert
&
Rosemarie

AIR CANADA

1957 Maurice & Elisabeth
with Albert's children
Kathy—Morris—Albert
Elisabeth & Bryan

Bryan, Maureen, Roberta & Scott Burns

3 Generations of Bernstein's 1982
Albert—Elizabeth—Rosemarie
with Bryan's children Scott & Roberta

4 Generations of Bernstein's 1979
Albert Burns-Maurice Bernstein-Bryan & Bryan's son Scott Burns

Irene Bernstein 1933 & Gerard Kerr 1932-1959

Gerard & Irene Kerr with Kim - Rosemarie & Albert Bernstein with Bryan Both men were in the RCAF at this point & flying F86 Saber jets

Irene & Gerard with 1st child Kim Kerr

Gerard & Irene Kerr with Kim Rosemarie & Albert Bernstein with Bryan

Gerard Jude Kerr 1932-1959—loved flying all his short life—chosen for the Golden Hawks Aerobatic flying Team in 1959 because of his flying skill

Irene Bernstein/Kerr ~ 1933 Family

Gerard Jude Kerr 1932-1959

Irene Ann Bernstein May 28, 1933
daughter of Morris & Elisabeth Bernstein

Irene's daughter Karen Elizabeth Kerr
with grandfather Maurice Bernstein

After Gerard's death, Maurice & Elisabeth
lived with Irene while Karen & Kim were
growing up

Wedding of Irene's son Kim Kerr to Jane Noiles July 3, 1992

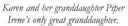

Karen and her granddaughter Piper
Irene's only great granddaughter.

Karen with daughter Jessica
Irene's granddaughter

Irene married Leonard "Lee" Davidson - April 1978

Minna Bernstein: 1897–1961

Minna (Bernstein) Corner at Coniston Railway Station

Minna Bernstein was born at home in Red River Parish, Louisiana, on February 10, 1897. She was only five months old when her father died.

Minna came to Canada with her mother in 1904, and while living in Espanola, Ontario, met Joseph Corner around 1910. The couple were married in Espanola Catholic Church on October 12, 1915.

Minna (Bernstein) & Joe Corner

Joe Corner worked as a papermaker at the mill in Espanola, and when the Ontario Paper Company, a subsidiary of the *Chicago Tribune*, opened a newsprint mill in Thorold, Ontario, the couple moved. Joe got a job starting as a back tender on the paper machines. He was very good at his job as well as being an excellent carpenter, having apprenticed at one time with a coffin maker. Their home in Thorold was in company housing known as Ontario Row.

Minna gave birth to their first child, Mary Louise, on August 5, 1916, in Hamilton, Ontario. A son, Lloyd, was born on June 11, 1918, and then three years later, there was another baby on the way. This time Minna's mother, Florence, acted as midwife when a second son was born at home in St. Catharines. Aubrey Joseph, a twin, was born on July 22, 1921. Unfortunately, his twin was born breeched and didn't survive childbirth.

Aubrey Corner at Coniston Railway Station

Minna (Bernstein) Corner with family members (Charlotte Chiswell on left)

Although Joe gambled, drank excessively, and chased woman (he had an illegitimate son by his neighbor), Minna stuck by him, and the couple stayed married and spent their entire life together.

His grandson, Gerry, remembers his grandfather with mixed emotions: "I never called him Grandpa, because he taught me to call him "my friend, Joe." I knew he was very good at his job as a machine tender because I worked with him for a while in my early work years. But Grandpa loved women, horse races, poker, and booze. On one occasion, my Grandmother Corner went to the local house of ill repute with a baseball bat and advised the rather large bouncer that either my grandfather came out or she was going in after him. They threw him out! One time when I was around five years of age and staying overnight with my grandparents my grandfather came home drunk. Not an unusual happening. They had a terrible fight that frightened me. When I went home and told my mother, I was only then allowed to go on day trips to my grandparents'. Later on, my brothers were also not allowed to go on overnight trips. Yet my grandparents stayed married until my grandmother's death, despite all the ups and downs. But my Grandpa Joe had some good qualities as well. When we lived at 98 Maple St., my Grandpa Joe built us a swing and teeter totter to play on. He built the frame out of two-inch steel pipe and cemented it well into the ground. I pity anyone who tried to remove it in future years."

I remember going to my Great-Aunt Minna's home as an eighteen-year-old teenager to help her with housework. She was a strong, cheerful, kind woman, and when I would come, she would bake the most amazing orange cake for me. Aunt Minna had heart problems and took Digitalis all the time. I believe she died in her sleep on July 20, 1961.

Joe remarried, but it was short lived, as he died on December 31, 1965, while he was on vacation in Florida. The couple are both buried in Victoria Lawn Cemetery in St. Catharines, Ontario.

Minna and Joseph Corner's Children

1. Mary Louise Corner, August 5, 1916–October 26, 1975: married Avila Michaud
2. Morris Lloyd Corner, June 11, 1918–December 16, 1937
3. Aubrey Joseph Corner, July 22, 1921–1965: married Phyllis Stringer

CB CB CB

Mary Louise Corner: 1916–1975

Mary Louise, born August 5, 1916, was Minna and Joe Corner's oldest child. When Louise Corner was a child, she contracted rheumatic fever, which severely damaged her mitral valve. Their doctor indicated that she would require a wheelchair to avoid any undue stress on her heart, nor would she be able to marry and have children. However, Louise was a strong-willed person. She refused to use a wheelchair, and despite suffering from uterine cancer in her early twenties and diabetes later in life, she went on to lead a full and rewarding life.

Louise married Avila George Michaud on June 15, 1936, and they were blessed with three boys: Gerrard, Morris (Maurice), and Mark. She is remembered by her children as being an excellent cook and completely devoted to her family. Louise was very artistic, teaching ceramics and china painting out of her home. I remember as a young teenager going to the Michaud home with my mother, who was taking lessons from Louise. The couple's creativity was non-stop; they even raised and sold a variety of hard to breed tropical fish. Louise was also active in the community as a board member of the Victorian Order of Nurses.

Avila worked as a papermaker and laborer at Thorold Paper Mill. On September 26, 1974, Avila George Michaud died, and a year later, on October 26, 1975, Louise also died. The couple are interred in Lake View Cemetery in Thorold, Ontario.

Louise & Avila Michaud's children

1. Gerrard (Gerry), May 6, 1937: married Marlene Bowman and had three children; second marriage to Sharon Wishlow after Marlene died

2. Mark, March 21, 1945: married Lois Devey and had three children

3. Lloyd, February 15, 1966–March 14, 2011: was a priest and clerk

Gerrard was fondly known as Gerry all his life. He has vivid memories of his great-grandmother, Florence Bernstein/Labelle, living with them, and of visiting his Grandmother Minna Corner, which has added to this book. In 1953, he was chosen as one of the thirty-two Queen's Scouts to represent Canada at the coronation of Queen Elizabeth II, carrying on to graduate from Notre Dame High School, Welland, in 1956. Gerry's career took him on the path of working at the Ontario Paper Company after high school for six years and then on to McKinnon Industry foundry, which was a subsidiary of G.M.

Canada. That was where Gerry got active with the United Auto Workers of American union, eventually becoming president of one of the largest local unions in Canada in 1979. He married Kathleen Rita Marleen Bowman on August 29, 1959, and the couple had four children. Marleen was born on July 11, 1937. After twenty-nine years of marriage, Marleen unfortunately died of cancer on September 4, 1988, leaving Gerry a widower. Two years on his own as a widower ended when Gerry re-married to Sharon Judith (Wishlow) McIntyre on June 21, 1991. They have six children and ten grandchildren between them. In 2021, the couple were enjoying retirement in a home they built in Tweed, Ontario.

Mark Anthony married Lois Devey on August 16, 1969, and they had three children prior to their divorce: Jason, David, and Demerise. Mark is a graduate of Interior Design at the Ontario College of Art and currently heads up the design department of the Art Shoppe in Toronto, Ontario. Mark left the Art Shoppe for a period and opened his own business. At the instigation of the Art Shoppe's owner, he eventually moved his business to offices at the Art Shoppe, where he was given all of their business and window designs in addition to serving his own clientele. Mark continues to live in Toronto with his partner, Will Ziegler, who operates one of the largest commercial door companies in Canada.

Lloyd became a Religious Brother with the Catholic Church as a teacher and administrator. He joined the Congregation of the Resurrection as a religious brother in August 1964 and took his perpetual vows on February 15, 1971. In 1980, he began his degree work at St. Jerome's University in religious studies and received his teacher's certificate at the University of Windsor in 1984, teaching at St. John's College in Brantford for nine years. After teaching, Lloyd completed his health care studies and did his practicum at St. Joseph's Hospital in Hamilton, giving him the perfect skill set to work at St. Pius Parish in the ministry of compassion, and then as administrator of St. Teresa Avila Parish in Elmira, Ontario. His many gifts included the ability to work with the elderly. Lloyd was a terrific uncle to the children of his brothers and had a keen sense of humor and practical view on things that helped him do his job well. As adults, the age difference between Lloyd and Gerrard lost its significance, and they regarded each other as best friends. Lloyd was his brother Gerry's best man when he married Sharon, and he spent many a happy weekend with Sharon and Gerry at their place in the country. Lloyd died in hospital in Kitchener on March 14, 2011, after a stroke.

CB CB CB

Louise (Corner) Michaud 1916-1975

Louise & Avila's Family
Back - Gerry - Mark
Lloyd with Avila & Louise Michaud in front

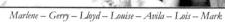

Marlene – Gerry – Lloyd – Louise – Avila – Lois – Mark

Mark – Gerry & Lloyd Michaud

Louise & Avila Michaud are buried in

Morris Lloyd Corner: 1918–1937

Louise's brother, Lloyd, born June 11, 1918, was said to have a good sense of humor. As a young man, he joined the Sea Cadets and loved to hunt and fish. He was engaged to be married to Helen Garner when he got blood poisoning as a result of pulling an ingrown hair. Lloyd died on December 16, 1937, and is interred at Victoria Lawn Cemetery in St. Catharines, Ontario. He was nineteen years old and engaged to be married at the time.

Aubrey Joseph Corner: 1921–1965

Aubrey, born July 22, 1921, was the youngest of Minna's children. He worked at the Ontario Paper Company and had a drinking problem like his father, Joe. He tried to emulate his old brother, Lloyd, in many ways, like taking up hunting. His nephew Gerry doesn't remember him being very good at it, resulting in Aubrey accidentally shooting his dog in the foot.

Marrying Phyllis Church Stringer on June 10, 1940, Aubrey is remembered as having been good to his five children. However, in mid-life he started doing some strange things, which were attributed to his drinking. He left his wife and remarried Elizabeth MacPherson, siring another child, John Shawn Corner, in 1957. About 1963 it was discovered that Aubrey had a brain tumor, which eventually killed him on February 25, 1964. It was felt that the tumor was probably responsible in part for his strange behavior earlier. Originally Aubrey was interred in Victoria Lawn Cemetery in St. Catharines, Ontario, but was later exhumed and moved to the Congregational Cemetery, Margaree Centre, Inverness, Nova Scotia, by his second wife. His son, John Shawn, became a corporal in the US Army and died in San Bruno, California.

Charlotte Imelda Bernstein: 1892–1960
(my grandmother)

Charlotte Imelda Bernstein, born at home in Red River Parish, Louisiana, on October 13, 1892, was my grandmother. After her father's death in 1897, her mother continued to live on their plantation on the Cane River for some time, but it's believed they may have moved to Coffee Springs, Alabama afterwards. When her mother came to Canada in 1904, Charlotte came with her as a twelve-year-old.

The family was living in Espanola, Ontario around 1907–1909. Charlotte got a job working in the Espanola Post Office and met my grandfather, Aubrey Reginald Chiswell, while working there. Aubrey was stationed at Webbwood, Ontario while working for the Canadian Pacific Railway. One of his duties was to take a hand pump rail car to Espanola to deliver and receive mail at the post office.

Aubrey & Charlotte Chiswell

Charlotte and Aubrey married on February 6, 1910, in St. John's Anglican Church in Webbwood, Ontario. Shortly afterwards, the young couple moved to Espanola, Ontario. This moved coincided with Aubrey Chiswell becoming a telegrapher at the Espanola station for the Canadian Pacific Railway. It was also there that their first child, my father, Albert Reginald Chiswell, was born on March 11, 1911.

In 1912, the family moved to Coniston, Ontario, where Aubrey was now working for Canadian Northern Railway System, which became part of the Canadian National Railway (CN) in 1919. He was the first station agent and telegrapher for the new Coniston Station. At first the station was merely a boxcar located on a siding, which also served as a home for the agent and his family. It was two years before a new building was erected with proper living quarters.

The couple had three more children: Ralph Morris Edison, born March 3, 1915; Edith Alberta, born November 2, 1919; and Audrey Ann, born June 27, 1931. All three children were born in the new station house in Coniston, Ontario.

Charlotte and Aubrey were very active in their church. When All Saints Anglican Church opened in Coniston in 1915, Aubrey served as treasurer, and Charlotte became an active member of the Women's Auxiliary. The ladies worked on various diocesan projects, including the encouragement of young people's activities, like dances and a Girls' Auxiliary of thirty-five girls at one time.

Charlotte's mother, Florence (Moseley/Bernstein) LaBelle, came to live with the family at the station house in 1920. It was while living with the family that Florence lost her sight to glaucoma while walking down the railway tracks.

Sometime after the formation of the United Church of Canada in 1925, Aubrey and Charlotte joined Saint Andrews United Church. Aubrey served as organist for the church for more than ten years. Charlotte worked on various church projects, such as fundraisers and children's programs. At times she organized and prepared entire church dinners.

In 1940, Aubrey entered Sudbury Memorial Hospital for minor surgery, believed to be an appendectomy. Unfortunately, complications developed during his recovery and caused his untimely death on September 28, 1940. He was interred in Park Lawn Cemetery, Sudbury, Ontario.

Within a short time, Charlotte and her youngest daughter, Audrey, had to move out of the station house to accommodate the new station agent. They moved to a house on Edwards Ave. in Coniston. Her mother, who was still living with them, moved to live with her other daughter, Minna Corner, in St. Catharines, Ontario.

Before 1950, Charlotte and Audrey Ann also moved to St. Catharines, where Audrey Ann married John Trotter on October 6, 1950 in Thorold, Ontario.

Charlotte eventually met and married a retired ship's captain known as Captain Dayton. Most of those people that remember Charlotte were too young to really know her when her first husband was alive. She is remembered as being quite a stern woman. However, when her niece, Mary Louise Corner/ Michaud, was hospitalized and forced to sell the family home to pay medical bills, it was Charlotte who took the family in for almost a year.

After Captain Dayton's death in late 1950s Charlotte returned to Coniston, Ontario to live with her son, Ralph. Not long after, on January 7, 1960, Charlotte died and is interred beside her husband in Park Lawn Cemetery in Sudbury, Ontario.

Charlotte and Aubrey Chiswell's Children

1. Albert Reginald, March 11, 1911–April 19, 1969 (my father)

2. Ralph Morris, March 3, 1915–February 11, 1982

3. Edith Albertina, November 2, 1919–October 13, 1985

4. Audrey Ann, June 27, 1931–March 31, 2003

Ralph & Peggy Chiswell

Margery & Albert Chiswell

Audrey Ann Chiswell & Jack Trotter

Edith Chiswell & Cecil Johnson

The next book I'm working on will be the Chiswell Family Story. Stay tuned and watch for it next year.

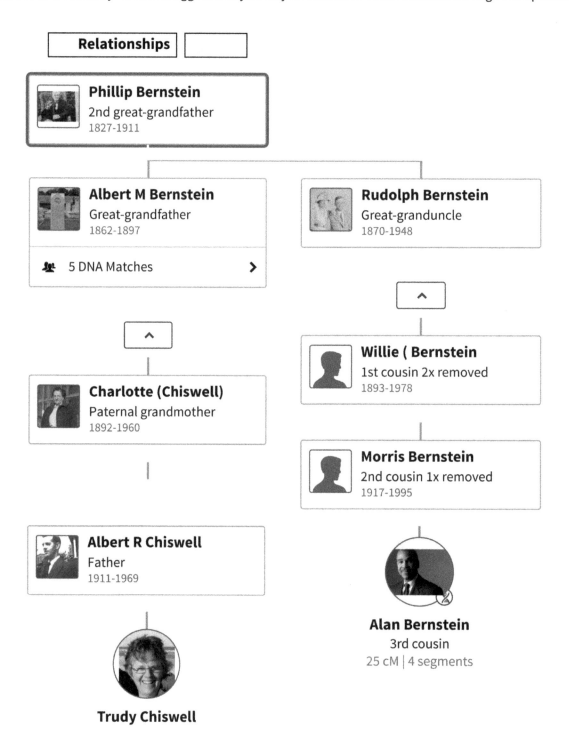

⟨ancestry⟩

ThruLines™ for Phillip Bernstein

ThruLines uses Ancestry® trees to suggest that you may be related to 6 DNA matches through Phillip Bernstein.

Relationships

Phillip Bernstein
2nd great-grandfather
1827-1911

Albert M Bernstein
Great-grandfather
1862-1897

👥 5 DNA Matches ❯

Rudolph Bernstein
Great-granduncle
1870-1948

⌃

Willie (Bernstein
1st cousin 2x removed
1893-1978

⌃

Charlotte (Chiswell)
Paternal grandmother
1892-1960

Morris Bernstein
2nd cousin 1x removed
1917-1995

Albert R Chiswell
Father
1911-1969

Alan Bernstein
3rd cousin
25 cM | 4 segments

Trudy Chiswell

African-American Descendants of Phillip & Rudolph Bernstein

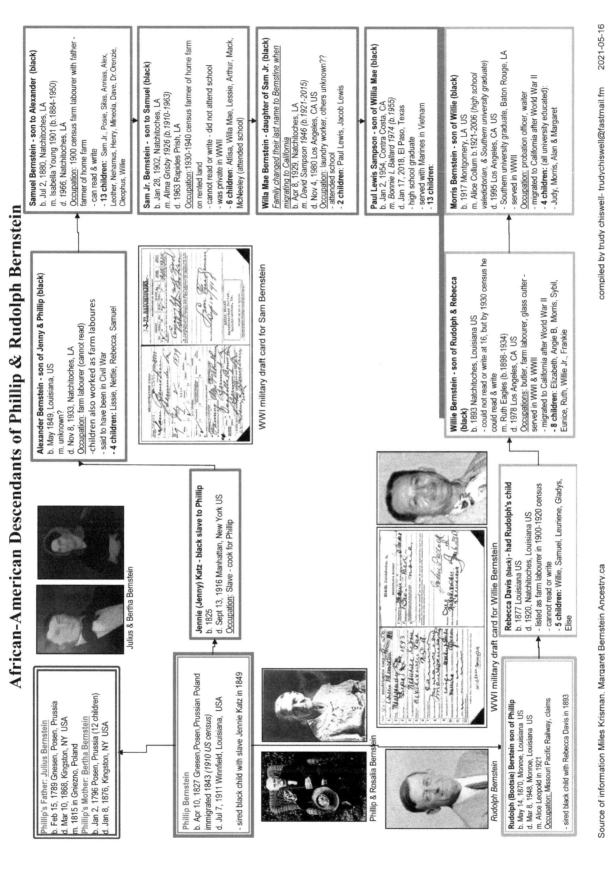

Phillip's Father: Julius Bernstein
b. Feb 15, 1789 Gnesen, Posen, Prussia
d. Mar 10, 1868, Kingston, NY USA
m. 1815 in Gniezno, Poland
Phillip's Mother: Bertha Bernstein
b. Jan 2, 1796 Posen, Prussia (12 children)
d. Jan 8, 1876, Kingston, NY USA

Julius & Bertha Bernstein

Phillip Bernstein
b. Apr 10, 1827 Gresen, Posen, Prussian Poland
immigrated 1843 *(1910 US census)*
d. Jul 7, 1911 Winnfield, Louisiana, USA
- sired black child with slave Jennie Katz in 1849

Jennie (Jenny) Katz - black slave to Phillip
b. 1825
d. Sept 13, 1916 Manhattan, New York US
Occupation: Slave - cook for Phillip

Phillip & Rosalia Bernstein

Rudolph Bernstein

WWI military draft card for Willie Bernstein

Rudolph (Bootsie) Berstein son of Phillip
b. May 14, 1870, Monroe, Louisiana US
d. Mar 8, 1948, Monroe, Louisiana US
m. Alice Leopold in 1921
Occupation: Missouri Pacific Railway, claims
- sired black child with Rebecca Davis in 1893

Rebecca Davis (black) - had Rudolph's child
b. 1877 Louisiana US
d. 1920, Natchitoches, Louisiana US
- listed as farm labourer in 1900-1920 census
- cannot read or write
- **5 children:** Willie, Samuel, Leuriene, Gladys, Elise

WWI military draft card for Sam Bernstein

Alexander Bernstein - son of Jenny & Phillip (black)
b. May 1849, Louisiana, US
m. unknown?
d. Nov 8, 1933, Natchitoches, LA
Occupation: farm labourer (cannot read)
-children also worked as farm laboures
- said to have been in Civil War
- **4 children:** Lissie, Nettie, Rebecca, Samuel

Samuel Bernstein - son to Alexander (black)
b. Jul 2, 1880, Natchitoches, LA
m. Isabella Young 1901 (b.1884-1950)
d. 1966, Natchitoches, LA
Occupation: 1900 census farm labourer with father - farmer of home farm
- can read & write
- **13 children:** Sam Jr., Posie, Silas, Annias, Alex, Leother, Nehamus, Henry, Mineola, Dave, Dr. Orenzie, Cleophus, Willie

Sam Jr. Bernstein - son to Samuel (black)
b. Jan 28, 1902, Natchitoches, LA
m. Alma Grisby 1926 (b.1910-1963)
d. 1963 Rapides Prish, LA
Occupation:1930-1940 census farmer of home farm on rented land
- cannot read or write - did not attend school
- was private in WWII
- **6 children:** Atiisa, Willa Mae, Lessie, Arthur, Mack, McNeeley (attended school)

Willa Mae Bernstein - daughter of Sam Jr. (black)
Family changed their last name to Bernsfine when migrating to California
b. Apr 8, 1929, Natchitoches, LA
m. David Sampson 1946 (b.1921-2015)
d. Nov 4, 1980 Los Angeles, CA US
Occupation: laundry worker, others unknown??
- attended school
- **2 children:** Paul Lewis, Jacob Lewis

Paul Lewis Sampson - son of Willia Mae (black)
b. Jan 2, 1954, Contra Costa. CA
m. Bonnie L Ballard 1974 (b.1955)
d. Jan 17, 2018, El Paso, Texas
- high school graduate
- served with Marines in Vietnam
- **13 children:**

Willie Bernstein - son of Rudolph & Rebecca (black)
b. 1893 Natchitoches, Louisiana US
- could not read or write at 16, but by 1930 census he could read & write
m. Ruth Eagles (b. 1898-1934)
d. 1978 Los Angeles, CA US
Occupations: butler, farm labourer, glass cutter - served in WWI & WWII
- migrated to California after World War II
- **8 children:** Elizabeth, Angie B. Morris, Sybil, Eunice, Ruth, Willie Jr., Frankie

Morris Bernstein - son of Willie (black)
b. 1917 Montgomery, LA US
m. Alice Collum b.1921-2006 *(high school valedictorian, & Southern university graduate)*
d. 1995 Los Angeles, CA US
Occupation: probation officer, waiter
- migrated to California after World War II
- **4 children:** *(all university educated):*
- Judy, Morris, Alan & Margaret

compiled by trudy chiswell- trudychiswell@fastmail.fm   2021-05-16

Source of information Miles Krisman, Margaret Bernstein Ancestry.ca

The African-American Bernstein Story

When I started investigating the Black side of the Bernstein family, I wasn't sure what I would find. As I dug further, I wanted to understand. Being raised in a Canadian community that had no racial division, I was totally ignorant of what it was like 170 years ago in my great-great-grandfather's time. We had Black people in our mostly white community, but I never thought of them as any different from me. Their skin color was different, but that was all. On my DNA profile in Ancestry and on 23&me, it came up with some people with the Bernstein last name, but they were black. I started gathering information from various people who lived and worked in Louisiana to get some insight. We knew from word-of-mouth family history handed down that Phillip Bernstein had sired a son with his mulatto slave, Jennie Katz, when he was twenty-eight years old in 1855, four years before he married. But that is all we knew. What happened to these people, and where did they go? Who were they?

I discovered that during the 1800s, a man's wealth was measured by how many slaves he owned. I couldn't find Phillip or Samuel Bernstein on the 1850 slave census, but they were in the 1860 one. In the 1860 slave census, Phillip has five slaves: a thirty-five-year-old Black female, a thirteen-year-old mulatto female, a seven-year-old Black male, a four-year-old mulatto female, and a one-year-old Black male. Samuel Bernstein has seven slaves on the 1860 slave census, so perhaps both brothers purchased slaves when they were building the new store in Winnfield in 1852, two years before it became the parish seat. Phillip's salves were mostly household and garden workers. By the 1870 census, the now "servants," after the emancipation of the slaves, had their names mentioned. They were thirty-five-year-old Jenny, a mulatto cook; eight-year-old Caroline, a mulatto; three-year-old Betsy, a mulatto; and fourteen-year-old Mary, a mulatto domestic servant. I can't find any record of Phillip and Jenny's fifteen-year-old son, Alexander, during this time. None of the Black slaves or servants could read or write. It's not known if these are the same servants listed on the slave census in 1860, but all four have Bernstein as their last name on the 1870 census. Black slaves took the last name of their slave owner after emancipation, so they weren't necessarily sired by the old slave owner. In her 1949 memoir, Phillip's daughter, Nettie, remembered an old slave of the family named Aunt Harriett. I couldn't find the servant Harriett in any of the census records, and after 1870, the only servant I found was Malissie Lenard in the 1910 census, who earned a wage.

I only found one census with Alexander, Phillip and Jennie's son. In the 1900 Natchitoches, Louisiana census, Alexander is listed as a farm laborer, renting house number six, and had never been unemployed that year. He is fifty-one years old, has been married twenty-five years, and has three girls and one boy, named Samuel. Alexander cannot read or write. I found it interesting that he named one of his children Nettie, the same as one of the daughters of his father, Phillip. That was the only census and records I could find for Alexander, but it gave me access into his descendants through his son, Samuel, to follow the family line.

Land was always very important to the blacks coming out of slavery. Claiming the soil as your own could get you killed in the Jim Crow South. At the same time, access to land was the path to self-reliance and financial independence. In 1865, US General William T. Sherman directed 400,000 acres of confiscated Confederate land to be distributed to formerly enslaved people. Under the mandate, named "40 Acres and a Mule," nearly 40,000 Black Americans were settled within six months. However, after Abraham Lincoln was assassinated, new President Andrew Johnson reneged on the promise, retuning the land to Confederate owners. There was redistribution of land but no reparations as promised to formerly enslaved people for lives of unpaid, involuntary service. So the descendants of Jennie continued to work farms for themselves but paid rent to land owner.[11]

By 1910, Alexander's son, Samuel, had married to twenty-five-year-old Isabella Young for nine years, with six children. Samuel had his sister, Rebecca, and her two children living with them. They are all listed as farm laborers working on a rented farm for themselves. None could read or write. Everything changed with Samuel, who was in WWI and WWII. They were still farm laborers but on their own rented land. Samuel had thirteen children in total, and two of the children and their wives lived on property close by. On the census up to 1940, many of the descendants listed their occupation as farm laborers, and it wasn't until after WWII that they moved away from it and migrated to California and Texas.

A descendent of Jennie and Alexander shared with me a little insight into what it was like for a Black family in the US South before they migrated to California.

Many blacks in the US South were not allowed to work as anything but farm laborers (sharecroppers) or house servants in the early years before WWII and for a while after. Those who tried to farm without an official white landlord, or start businesses, were often put into "the lease" or killed in their homes by night riders.

On the boys' return from WWII, everything changed for the family. This is the generation that started to be educated and changed the direction of their lives. The men returning from war had been treated differently overseas, and on their return, realized that they would never be accepted in Louisiana because they were black. The Black men who served and fought for their country were then considered "uppity" when they wore their uniform in public after the war. Some were killed. Wearing the uniform was seen as a direct challenge to the white heroes of the war. Most of them decided to move to California and start a new life. After WWII, the Black Bernsteins asked themselves two questions before deciding to re-locate.

1. *Why are we in Louisiana where white people are never going to give an inch more freedom to Blacks?*

2. *Why are we carrying around this Jewish sounding name when we are not Jewish?*

Most of the brothers changed the spelling of their last name to **Bernstine** *and moved to the Bay Area of California. There are Black Bernsteins and Bernstines in California, Texas, and Iowa mostly. In their new life in California, some became bus drivers, car salesmen, a pastor, and other Bernstine men played college sports.* [12]

Explanation of 1850 & 1860 U.S. Federal Census – Slave Schedules

During the 1850 and 1860 United States Federal Census, enslaved individuals were recorded separately in what were called slave schedules. This database provides details about those persons, including age, sex, and color, but unfortunately, most schedules omit personal names. Some enumerators did, however, list the given names of enslaved people—particularly those over one hundred years of age—which are generally found in the "name of slave owners" column. The Census Bureau started collecting birth dates in 1902, and the National Office of Vital Statistics took over birth certificates nationally in 1946. Before this time, it was family Bibles (the Bernsteins' family Bible entries are at the end of the book) and church records that recorded births, but this did not include the blacks and slaves of the time. There were no birth certificates for Black children back then. Later, they had to go to a government seat and swear an affidavit to get a record of their birth when they needed it for applying for work or benefits. They had to have a person vouch for them that the data was correct. [13]

Arnold Bernstein—A Different Man

Some of our ancestors in the early years didn't believe in slavery or abuse of Blacks, as seen in Arnold Bernstein story. Arnold strove for racial equality and improved race relations in his part of Louisiana during his twenty-year term as mayor of Monroe Louisiana. This was a time when lynchings and extreme violence against African Americans was at its height, and he was determined to put a stop to it. Mayor Bernstein considered himself to be a minority member, since he was Jewish. He refused the Ku Klux Klan a permit to march in parades in downtown Monroe during the 1920s. Mayor Bernstein paid for the college education of one of Ouachita parish's esteemed educators, Henry Carroll (namesake of Carroll High School). Henry Carroll was of Black heritage and became a leading educator in Munroe, a spokesman for Blacks, a teacher, a football coach, and eventually the principal during the 1940s. He made such an impression on the community that the high school was named after him in 1953. Mayor Bernstein also endorsed the business of African Americans in Monroe, most notably the medical practice of Dr. J.T. Miller and Dr. J.C. Roy.

In my research with DNA, I found that I had a connection with Alan Bernstein, a Black businessman, who is the Director of Client Solutions for a marketing company in Los Angeles, California, USA. It took quite a long time to build up trust before Alan, his brother and sisters would talk to me, but it was a real education for me. The following story is from Alan's younger sister, Margaret, a writer who wrote a story for a Chicago newspaper about the shock of discovering her roots from a white slave owner.

Unfolding Secrets

Old records & modern genetics reveal painful truth about one Black woman's roots

Published article in *The Plain Dealer* newspaper March 17, 2006
By Margaret Bernstein: great grandchild of Rudolph Bernstein
margaretbernstein@sbcglobal.net

American history has been cruel to blacks. Of course I know that.

But I feel a fresh heartbreak as I attach the name of a slave owner to a branch in my family tree. As I, a black woman, review stunning DNA test results that show 56 percent of my ancestry is Indo-European, and only 37 percent is sub-Saharan African. As I pay spiritual homage to my unknown female ancestors who, during slavery, most likely served as sexual property, giving birth to three children classified as "mulatto" in the 1870 census.

I'm not completely surprised to find this information. It's written in my light skin. Imprinted in my surname. Everyday clues to a painful past. But new advances in genealogical technology are enabling me and other blacks to study our history in more detail. With DNA analysis, online access to census data and improved indexing of black records, it's becoming possible to push past the roadblocks that kept us from learning who our forebears were. These dramatic advances were spotlighted in the recent PBS special "African American Lives," which some say is sparking a level of enthusiasm in black genealogy to rival the phenomenon of Alex Haley's "Roots."

The U.S. Census didn't count blacks until 1870. Before that, we were possessions, enumerated like cows and horses. No names. Just ages and gender, listed on slave schedules were listed.

Like many blacks, I knew the names of relatives born in the past century, but couldn't go back much further. As a race, our history hasn't been passed down, mainly because slaves weren't allowed to read and write, they weren't given last names and their families often were split up. A child sold away from his parents would know little about his heritage.

It also can be a genealogical dead end when one encounters a child fathered by a white man. Just finding out the father's name can be difficult. Elders often weren't told the details or may not want to rehash them. Blacks and whites of earlier generations may have had children together but rarely lived in the same home, which means there is no census record linking mother and father. I know of three such shadowy unions between black women and white men that predate 1900 in my family tree—which explains in part why I have such a significant amount of European blood. I believe there are others, although I can't begin to trace them due to the paucity of pre-Civil War records for blacks.

But I have a copy of my paternal grandfather's birth certificate. My family has long known the full name of his white father. When I plugged that name, Rudolph Bernstein, into census pages available online at ancestry.com, I learned that his family's roots go back to Germany. I actually lost my breath when I discovered a page that showed Rudolph's father Phillip, owned five slaves in Louisiana in 1860: a 35-year-old woman and four children, two of them "mulatto."

Sandi Craighead, co-founder of the African American Genealogical Society of Cleveland, helped me to understand the world into which my grandfather was born in 1893. In the South, until at least 1900, it was common to find white men having children with black women, she said. Sometimes it was a clear-cut case of rape; other times it was a decision of financial survival for the women who tended to work as domestics, earning little money. A white man might provide money or assistance for a black paramour, Craighead said. Just because slavery ended in 1865 didn't mean blacks were suddenly free of old social patterns, she explained. "Once Reconstruction was over, it was back to the same old games, only nobody was called a slave ... A lot of these black women without any protection, they did a lot of stuff just trying to stay alive. And it's sad. They became pregnant. It's common to find these kinds of situations."

My anger started to rise as I uncovered similar scenarios on my mother's side. Where there no white men in the South who didn't feel entitled to take advantage of black women sexually? And how on earth am I going to explain all this to my young son and daughter?

There's not much I can say to sugar-coat the brief union between my great-grandmother, Rebecca Davis and Rudolph Bernstein, the father of her child. Census reports show that she lived as a single mother, and had to move in with an uncle after giving birth to my grandfather. Everything my family knows about our white great grandfather wouldn't fill a thimble. My father remembered seeing Rudolph only once, during childhood, when Rudolph appeared on their porch asking for his "N....r son."

I asked Ann Sindelar, Western Reserve Historical Society reference librarian, to show me how to use census documents to compare the lifestyle of my white great-grandfather with that of his black son. We found that in 1930, both were living in Louisiana, in neighboring counties or "parishes." My great-grandfather lived in Monroe, where news articles show that his brother, Arnold was enjoying a third term as the city's mayor. Rudolph Bernstein, 59, resided with his white wife and daughter in a white neighborhood where many were employed as broker, bookkeepers and bankers. A railroad claims agent, he owned one of the most expensive houses on the street.

My grandfather, on the other hand, was working as a butler in a private home. At age 37, Willie Bernstein lived in a Shreveport apartment with his wife and five kids, in a neighborhood of blacks working subservient jobs as laundresses, cooks and porters. His mother had died 10 years earlier.

James K. Jeffrey, genealogy collections specialist at the Denver Public Library, expects that blacks will feel a range of emotions as they start digging into their histories. It's best to use the facts, no matter how hurtful, to gain an appreciation for the strength of one's ancestors, he said. He helped me imagine what life must have been like for Milly Green, on my mother's side, who gave birth to the child of a white farmer in Mississippi five years after slavery ended. She was 18, poor and likely alone, separated from her biological family. Was she treated like a queen by the man who fathered her child or like a slave? It is impossible to know for sure, although I suspect is was the latter, given the year and place.

Jeffrey said it seems fair to surmise that "she was a strong woman who had that child and another after that. She was a woman who after the ravages of slavery was able to pick herself up and make her own life. She found her strength from deep within herself," he said. "That is what you take pride in."

A mere 60 years after slavery ended, Milly's grandson – my maternal grandfather – was steering my family to middle-class stability in Mississippi. The head of a deeply spiritual household, he was a devoted husband and father who worked hard to send his daughters to college in the 1930s. He had to send them to a black college, of course. No sense in waiting for colleges in the South to integrate. "Ole Miss" refused to admit a black student until 1962. Just two generations from slavery, miracles can occur. I see that pattern repeatedly in the new map of my family that I've constructed. Ancestry.com helped me fill in a few last names of relatives born into slavery that I never knew before – and other valuable facts.

A postscript, written in March 2021:

I wrote the preceding article fifteen years ago. It's been a happy surprise for me to connect with "Cousin trudy" in 2021 and to have her fill in the blanks of our shared ancestry. As a sixty-one-year-old Black woman, I never thought that I would ever strike up a relationship with the descendants of my Jewish great-great-grandfather, Phillip Bernstein, even though four generations later I still retain his surname.

I want to recommend to both my Black relatives and my newfound white and Jewish ones that they read *Caste: The Origins of Our Discontent* by Isabel Wilkerson. It is absolutely the best, most eye-opening book about race relations that I have read in the past year. She draws many parallels between the treatment of Jews in Nazi Germany and that of African-Americans during slavery and after. Both groups were stigmatized and subjected to a rigid "caste system" that dehumanized them and placed them at the bottom of the social hierarchy.

Wilkerson writes that Jewish immigrants, when arriving in the United States a century or more ago, had the choice of rejecting the lowest caste of American society, which was occupied by Blacks, or "making common cause" with them. I believe that in nineteenth-century Louisiana, these were the exact dynamics at play when my Black great-grandmother and Jewish great-grandfather had occasion to meet. It was this shared placement at the bottom of the social order that caused their worlds to collide. Historical records don't give any clues as to the nature of their relationship, but the one thing that I know is that I had the great luck to grow up in an exceptionally loving and closely knit family of Black Bernsteins. What's unquestionable about the union of Rebecca Davis and Rudolph Bernstein is that it produced a magnificent and hardy branch on the family tree. And it continues to flourish today. [14]

Willie Bernstein 1893-1978
Rudolph Bernstein's son

World War I draft registration for Willie Bernstein

World War II draft registration for Willie Bernstein

Affidavit of Birth
PERSONAL AND STATISTICAL PARTICULARS ABOUT CHILD

Full name of child ___ Willie Bernstein

Date of birth ___ September 2, 1893 ___ At ___ A. M. / P. M. Sex ___ male

Place of Birth ___ Natchitoches, Natchitoche Parish, Louisiana

PERSONAL AND STATISTICAL PARTICULARS ABOUT CHILD'S FATHER

Full name of father ___ Bootsie Bernstein

Residence at child's birth ___ Natchitoches, Louisiana

Age at child's birth ___ 26 ___ years. Color or race ___ white

Birthplace ___ Louisiana

Occupaion at child's birth ___ Lawyer

PERSONAL AND STATISTICAL PARTICULARS ABOUT CHILD'S MOTHER

Full maiden name of mother ___ Rebecca Davis

Residence at child's birth ___ Natchitoches, Louisiana

Age at child's birth ___ 16 ___ years. Color or race ___ negro

Birthplace ___ Louisiana

Occupation at child's birth ___ Housewife

This is the ___ first ___ child born to this mother.

Including this child, there were then ___ one ___ children of this mother living.

STATE OF ___ California

County of ___ Los Angeles ___ }ss.

I hereby certify that I am the ___ Brother-in-law ___ of the above mentioned child and that the facts and data as alleged are true and correct to the best of my knowledge and belief and that I am a native citizen of ___ Louisiana

a citizen or naturalization of ___
(Cross out the words that do not apply)

Earl Eagles
Affiant

1223 California Ave.,
Long Beach, Calif.
Address

SUBSCRIBED AND SWORN to before me this ___ 19th ___ day of ___ October ___, 19 43

Verne Chiswell
Notary Public in and for the County of

Los Angeles ___, State of ___ California

My Commission Expires April 22, 1946

Birth Certificates in the USA were not given out until 1900. Black children were not in the family bible or church records as the white children. They had to later go with documentation and representatives to vouch for them to obtain an affidavit of birth.

REGISTRAR'S REPORT
DESCRIPTION OF REGISTRANT

RACE		HEIGHT (Approx.)	WEIGHT (Approx.)	COMPLEXION	
White		5'8"	148	Sallow	
		EYES	HAIR	Light	
Negro	✓	Blue	Blonde	Ruddy	
		Gray	Red	Dark	
Oriental		Hazel	Brown	Freckled	
		Brown ✓	Black ✓	Light brown	✓
Indian		Black	Gray	Dark brown	
			Bald		
Filipino					

Other obvious physical characteristics that will aid in identification ___ none

I certify that my answers are true; that the person registered has read or has had read to him his own answers; that I have witnessed his signature or mark and that all of his answers of which I have knowledge are true, except as follows:

none to my knowledge

Zurline Baker
(Signature of registrar)

Register for Local Board ___ 1 ___ Caddo ___ La.
(Number) (City or county) (State)

Date of registration ___ April 26, 1942

LOCAL BOARD No. 3
CADDO PARISH
COURT HOUSE
SHREVEPORT, LA.
(STAMP OF LOCAL BOARD)

*July 15, 1978—buried in Cypress,
Orange County, California*

Willie Bernstein's Family 1893-1978

Rudolph Bernstein's son

Willie Bernstein and his children—son Morris is serving in WWII at the time
Willie Bernstein Sr—Elizabeth Ford—Sybil James—Eunice Davis—Ruth Bernstein—Willie Bernstein Jr—Frankie Wise

Willie Bernstein's son Morris and his children
Back row LtoR: Morris Jr.—Judy—Margaret—Alan & Front row: Alice & Morris Sr.

So this is the end of the Bernstein story of my family tree and the beginning of the Chiswell story. The Mosely line of my Great-Grandmother Florence (Moseley) Bernstein's origin is also coming after the Chiswell story. I will be doing five family lines altogether: Bernstein, Chiswell, Maves, Daley, and Moseley in the future. Watch for these next families in their own book coming out soon.

CB CB CB

SOURCE DOCUMENTS
OF THE
BERNSTEIN FAMILY

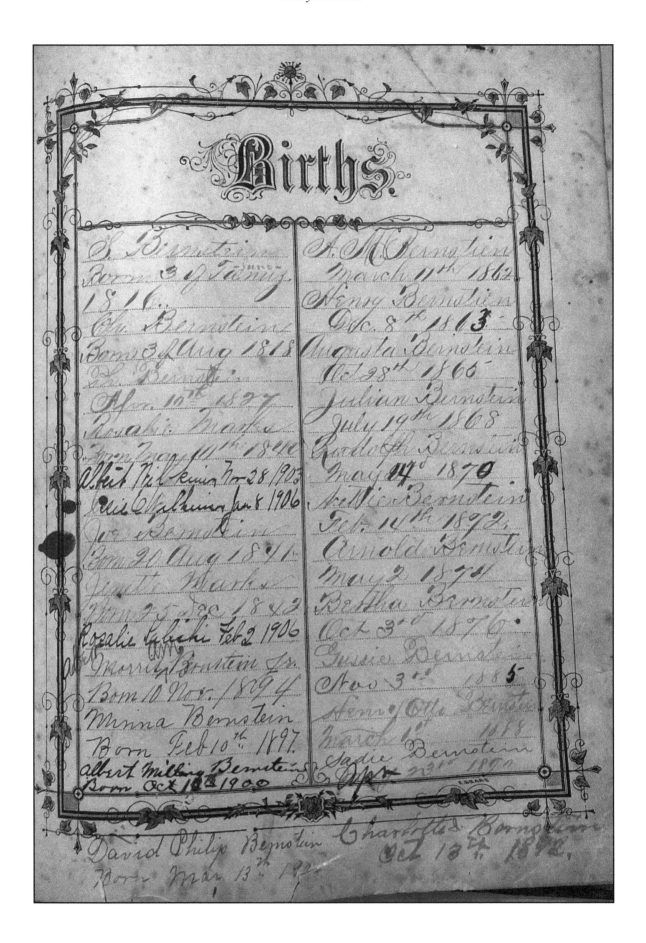

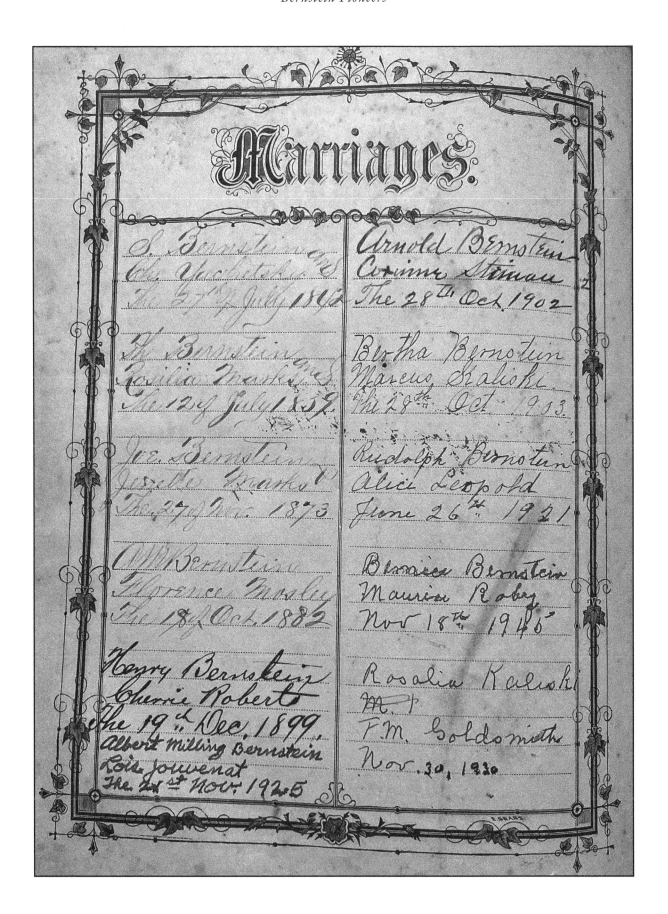

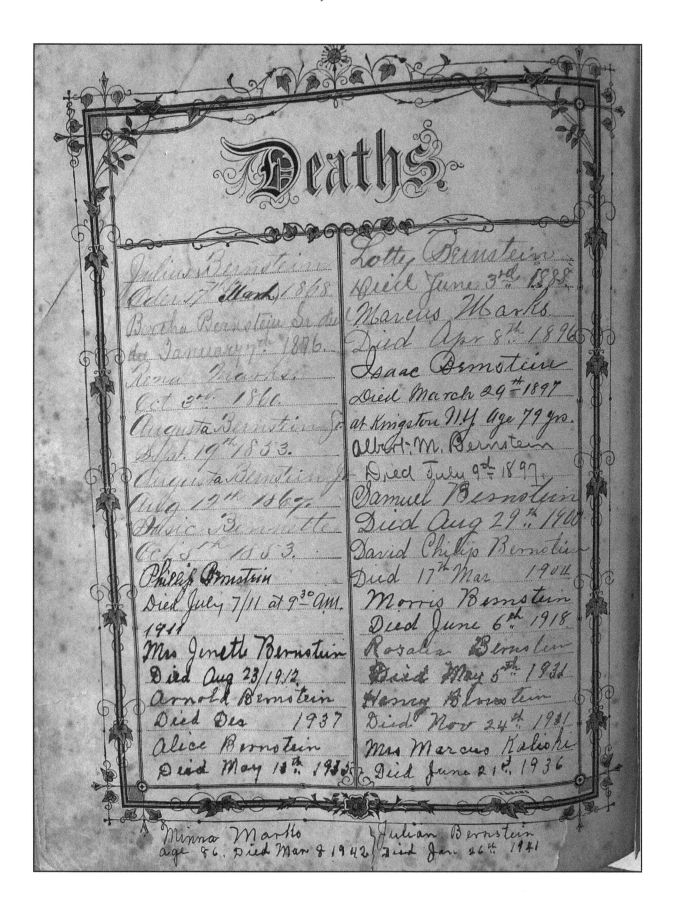

Deaths.

Julius Bernstein
October 7th March 1868

Bertha Bernstein Sr. die
die January 7th 1896

Rena Marks
Oct 2nd 1860

Augusta Bernstein Sr.
Sept 19th 1853.

Augusta Bernstein Jr.
July 19th 1867.

Music Bennette
Oct 5th 1853.

Philip Bernstein
Died July 7/11 at 9:30 A.M.
1911

Mrs Jenette Bernstein
Died Aug 23/1912

Arnold Bernstein
Died Des   1937

Alice Bernstein
Died May 18th 1935

Lotty Bernstein
Died June 3rd 1888

Marcus Marks
Died Apr 8th 1896

Isaac Bernstein
Died March 29th 1897
at Kingston N.Y Age 79 yrs.

Albert M. Bernstein
Died July 9th 1897

Samuel Bernstein
Died Aug 29th 1900

David Philip Bernstein
Died 17th Mar 1904

Morris Bernstein
Died June 6th 1918

Rosalia Bernstein
Died May 5th 1931

Henry Blonstein
Died Nov 24th 1931

Mrs Marcus Kaliski
Died June 21st 1936

Minna Marks
age 86. Died Mar 8 1942

Julian Bernstein
Died Jan 26th 1941

Bits from Bernstein Family Bible

Births

Henry Milling Bernstein Dec. 20, 1950 Son of Henry and Betty Jane Bernstein

John Morris Gulledge Aug. , 1951 Son of Cherry and Fred Gulledge

James Scott Bernstein Nov. 1, 1953 Son of Henry and Betty Jane Bernstein

Cherry Layden Gulledge Feb. , 1955 Daughter of Cherry and Fred Gulledge

Frederick Lamar Gulledge Jr. Dec. 25, 1960 Son of Cherry and Fred L. Gulledge

Katherine Goldsmith Mar. 6, 1965 Daughter of Jay and Linda Goldsmith

William Kennet Goldsmith Mar. 27, 1967 Son of Jay and Linda Goldsmith

Albert Eugene Gulledge May 1967 Son of Cherry and Fred Gulledge

Lois Henry Gulledge Aug 1968 Daughter of Cherry and Fred Gulledge

Becki Anne Roby May 28, 1973 Daughter of Irving and Linda Roby

Marriages

Henry Bernstein Jr and Marie Collins Blackman   July 10, 1948

Henry Bernstein III and Betty Jane Duke   August 19, 1949

Cherry Louise Bernstein and Fred L. Gulledge   August 11, 1950

Jay Kennet Goldsmith and Linda Collet   August 17, 1963

Philip Irving Roby and Sharyn Marcovitz   February 20, 1972

Deaths

Cherry Roberts Bernstein in Monroe, La.

Nettie Bernstein "Lutta" in Winnfield, La.

Albert Milling Bernstein in Monroe, La.   May 29, 1967

R. Rudolph Bernstein age 78 Died Mar. 8th 1948 —
Mrs Corinne Steiman Bernstein —
wife of Arnold Bernstein —
Died Feb 9th 1955, at
Monroe, Louisiana.

Bernstein Family Bible bits

Rosalia Kaliski
Born Feb 2nd 1906

Henry ~~Charles~~ Bernstein Jr
Born Oct 31st 1906.

Henry

Bernice Bernstein
Born Mar. 28th 1922

Henry (Teddy) Bernstein
Born Sept 25th 1926

Cherry Louise Bernstein
Born Thursday Dec. 20th 1928.

Jay Kennet Goldsmith
June 24th 1941
Son of Rosalia Kaliski
F. M. Goldsmith
Philip Irving Roby
Aug 14th 1947
Son of Bernice Bernstein
Maurice Roby
Alice Roby
Born Oct 20-1948
Daughter of Bernice Bernstein
& Maurice Roby

Death Certificates

Rosalia Marks Bernstein - May 5, 1931

Morris Bernstein - June 6, 1918

Death Certificates

Nettie Bernstein - November 5, 1959

Julian Bernstein - January 26, 1941

A

HISTORY *of* LOUISIANA

Wilderness—Colony—Province
Territory—State—People

———

BY

HENRY E. CHAMBERS

Member, The Louisiana Historical Society, The Mississippi Valley Historical Association,
and the American Historical Association.
Author of A School History of the U. S.; A Higher History of the U. S.; West Florida
and Its Relation to the Historical Cartography of the U. S.; Louisiana,
Past and Present; The Territory of Orleans and Mod-
ern Louisiana (The South in the Building of
the Nation); The Constitutional
History of Hawaii; Mis-
sissippi Valley
Beginnings

———

VOLUME III

———

PUBLISHERS
THE AMERICAN HISTORICAL SOCIETY, Inc.
Chicago and New York
1925

ENDNOTES

1 Sources of Information
  - Sources of Information for entire book
  - ancestry.ca
  - findagrave.com
  - 23&me.com – genealogy dna
  - https://www.fold3.com – military records
  - https://www.history.com/topics/religion/judaism
  - Miles Krisman's research on the Bernstein family in the 1990s. Many have used Miles's research since.
  - Lou Harrison the granddaughter of Sadie Bernstein Larocque
  - Gerry Michaud the grandson of Minna Bernstein Corner
  - Phillip Roby the grandson of Rudolph Bernstein
  - Henry Milling Bernstein great-grandson of Henry Bernstein Sr.
  - Historian Sandra Blate of Temple B'nai Israel, Monroe Louisiana.
  - Excerpts from: *Natchitoches Parish, Biographical & Historical Memoirs of Northwest Louisiana* (Nashville & Chicago, The Southern Publishing Company, 1890)
  - Henry E. Cambers : *A History of Louisiana —Wilderness —Colony —Province —Territory —State —People* (The American Historical Society Inc., Chicago & New York 1925)
  - Nettie Bernstein, at seventy-eight years old, daughter of Phillip Bernstein: (Personal Memoirs, transposed by Henry Jr. Bernstein's secretary December 27, 1949)

2 web site sources: https://www.familysearch.org – https://www.4crests.com – https://www.genesreunited.co.uk – Dictionary of American Family Names ©2013, Oxford University Press

3 1- Hugh Chisholm, "Gnesen": 1911- Encyclopedia Britannica, Vol 12 – https://www.en.wikisource.org/wiki.1911_encyclopedia_britannica/Gnesen

4 *Article by James Andrews: Lawyer, Genealogist, Geneticist, California USA:* james_andrews555@yahoo.com

5 Dhale & Eugene F. Love: *LOOKING BACK—Winn Parish 1852-1986 - History of Winn Parish, book 2* (Shreveport Memorial Library, Shreveport Louisiana, USA)

6 Excerpts from: *Natchitoches Parish, Biographical & Historical Memoirs of Northwest Louisiana* – (Nashville & Chicago, The Southern Publishing Company, 1890)

7 Article from The Southern Sentinel newspaper, Winnfield, LA)

8 Article from The Southern Sentinel newspaper, Winnfield, LA

9 Dhale & Eugene F. Love: *LOOKING BACK – Winn Parish 1852-1986 - History of Winn Parish, book 2* (Shreveport Memorial Library, Shreveport Louisiana, USA)

10 Vetrans Affairs web site - https://www.veterans.gc.ca/eng/remembrance/memorials/canadian-virtual-war-memorial/detail/80002789 (last accessed March 2021)

11 Debora Simmons, History Executive Editor Article: *Why Owning the Land Matters* – (Nation Geographic web site) https://www.nationalgeographic.com (last accessed March 2021)

12 Kristl Tyler – descendant of Jennie Katz and Alexander Bernstein

13 *Explanation of Slave Schedule from Ancestry.ca*

14 Margaret Bernstein: *Unfolding Secrets* (Arts & Life, The Plain Dealer newspaper, March 17, 2006- author contribution)

CPSIA information can be obtained
at www.ICGtesting.com
Printed in the USA
BVHW021446090222
628492BV00016B/1665